SCHOLASTIC

W9-AYN-963

20 Week-by-Week Word Family Packets

An Easy System for Teaching the Top 120 Word Families to Set the Stage for Reading Success

by Lisa Fitzgerald McKeon

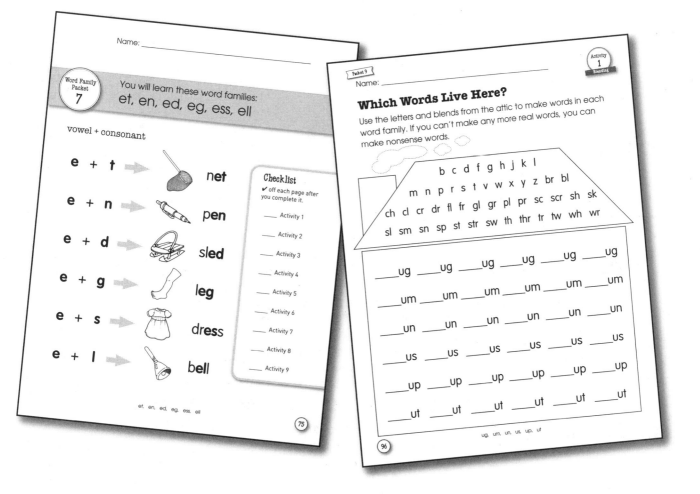

New York • Toronto • London • Auckland • Sydney
New Delhi • Mexico City • Hong Kong • Buenos Aires

Teaching *Resources*

Dedication

for Mom and Dad
and their countless bedtime stories

–L.

Cover design by Jorge Namerow
Interior design by Gerard Fuchs/Grafica, Inc.
Interior illustrations by Maxie Chambliss, Steve Cox, Gerard Fuchs, James Graham Hale,
Doug Jones, Anne Kennedy, Ka-Yeon Kim, Brian LaRossa, and Mike Moran

ISBN-10: 0-439-92923-7
ISBN-13: 978-0-439-92923-3

11 12 13 14 15 16   20 19

Contents

Introduction

A Note From the Author

For as long as I can remember, the first page of a new book has been full of promise for me. I can recall the excitement I felt as a child each time I walked home from the library, knowing that a newly acquired treasure was safely tucked away in my backpack and just waiting to be opened up. It was, in a word, magical. As an adult, things haven't changed much. Books continue to transport me to new places, to new states of mind, and to new experiences. Literacy has been, without a doubt, one of the most powerful tools I have been given in my life.

And so perhaps it is no surprise that I chose literacy as the focus of my adult career. As a reading specialist, I assist young children in their acquisition of the deep, well-rooted literacy skills that have served me so well throughout my life. There are, of course, many skills involved in becoming a fluent, accomplished reader, but in my professional opinion, learning word families is the ideal way to begin the process. When children study word families (words related to one another by their ending sounds and common spelling patterns), they learn to recognize the similarities between words. This, in turn, leads to increased sight and spelling vocabulary—which then leads to increased fluency as both a reader and a writer.

In the pages of this book, I am proud to share the methods and activities I've developed to help young children get their start on the road to reading success. Time and time again, I've seen children who engage in these activities make great strides in their literacy learning, not only by acquiring the concrete skills they need, but also by acquiring a love of reading itself. The world of books is indeed a magical one, and I hope this book will help you experience a new kind of magic: the sheer joy that comes from seeing a child discover the endless wonders of the written word.

Enjoy!

Lisa

Lisa Fitzgerald McKeon

Why Word Families?

Teaching word families is an essential component of any literacy program. Since learning word families involves recognizing words that end with the same sound and spelling pattern, studying them builds phonemic awareness of rhyming sounds and also increases children's sight word vocabulary. The activities in this book support young readers by teaching them a variety of phonograms (letters in the word family that stand for the common sound), and the more phonograms children can recognize, the more words they can read and spell. Think about it: If a reader knows the word *cat*, it is much easier to recognize the words *bat, rat, sat*, and *mat*.

Research has repeatedly shown that direct phonics instruction is an important part of literacy learning, and that word family instruction is a highly valuable way to teach sound-spelling relationships. An astounding number of the words children will encounter in their reading fall into common word families, and within these families, words that use the same cluster of letters are almost always pronounced the same way. Direct instruction of these common relationships helps children learn to detect patterns in words and increases their automaticity—the ability to recognize words on sight, without having to decode them (or in other words, sound them out).

Automaticity, in turn, leads to even greater gains, because as children's word-recognition skills improve, so does their comprehension. Why? Because sounding out a word takes up time and brainpower. The faster children can recognize words, and the less energy they need to expend in order to do it, the more there is left over to devote to understanding the meaning of the words. Comprehending ideas is, of course, the ultimate goal in becoming a fluent reader—and learning word families is an essential step toward reaching that goal.

About This Book

Twenty Week-by-Week Word Family Packets is the product of my professional research and experience as a reading specialist. It is designed to provide you with a full range of fundamental phonetic and phonemic activities to support emerging and early readers. The activities in each packet, which have been used successfully with my own students, systematically introduce and reinforce 120 of the most essential word families. Each activity is presented in a simple layout that is both easy to understand and fun to complete, promising to engage even the most reluctant readers.

The book is organized into 20 packets of study. Each packet begins with a page that introduces six new word families, followed by nine engaging activity sheets that help children practice the word families. The activities are also structured to address several important core reading skills (see About the Activity Skills, page 9). Plus, they're designed to appeal to a variety of learning styles to ensure you can reach each and every child. The program is flexible, so you can complete the exercises in order or pick and choose the particular skills you'd like to target (see Instructional Options, page 12).

Perhaps most important, the sheets are designed to be quick and easy to use—just copy a set and you're ready to go! Because the directions are clear and easy to understand, they're ideal for independent work as well as whole-class instruction (see Grouping Options, page 11).

About the Activity Skills

Each packet of activities is structured to give children repeated practice with several core reading skills. These skills are focused on specific aspects of phonetic analysis, spelling, and comprehension, and each one contributes to emergent readers' literacy learning. Finding activities that focus on a particular skill is a snap—the skill label is listed on the top right-hand corner of each activity page. Following are descriptions of each skill, plus tips for leading children toward mastery.

◆ **Previewing:** The first page of each packet allows children to preview the sounds and spellings they will learn in the upcoming activities. Children are introduced to the letters that make up each phonogram sound and given a word example as well as a picture for each one. The packet openers also act as a tool for self-monitoring. On the right side of the page, children will see a list of all the activity pages in the packet. Encourage children to check off each activity as they complete it.

◆ **Blending:** Sound blending, also called *sound synthesis*, is the process of putting individual sounds together in order to form a new sound or word. The first activity in each packet invites children to blend an initial consonant or consonant cluster with a phonogram, or word ending, to create a complete word (for example, *b* + *at* = *bat*; *cl* + *ap* = *clap*). Depending on students' levels, some children may benefit from the use of manipulatives to complete this type of activity. You can provide children with letter tiles to help them try out different consonant beginnings and word endings. Another option is to write the target phonograms for the packet on index cards, and write different initial letters on additional cards. Children can try out different combinations by laying the cards side by side.

◆ **Isolating:** The act of attending to individual sounds within words is called *isolating*. In this book you'll find three different types of isolating activities.

   Basic Isolating: This type of activity helps children recognize that sounds occur in different positions within words—that is, a particular sound can appear at the beginning, middle, or end of a word. For example, children are asked where in the word they hear the *v* in *van* (beginning), the *a* in *tag* (middle), and the *t* in *bat* (end). Point out that children can say each word aloud to help them hear where the sound occurs.

   Isolating Through Segmentation: Segmenting refers to the act of isolating the sounds in a spoken word by separately pronouncing each one in order. This type of activity encourages children to determine how many phonemes (or individual sounds) they hear in a particular word. For instance, the word *at* has two sounds: the vowel short *a* and the consonant *t*. The word *cap* has three sounds: the consonant *c*, the vowel short *a*, and the consonant *p*. Encourage students to read each word aloud slowly, taking a short pause between each sound. Explain that the number of sounds in a word does not always equal the number of letters. You may want to review digraphs (such as *sh* and *th*), diphthongs (such as *ou* and *ow*), and vowel teams (such as *ea* and *ee*) before children begin, pointing out that two letters put together can make one sound.

Isolating Through Cloze: This type of activity uses the cloze method, inviting children to choose the correct letter(s) to complete a word in the context of a sentence. For instance, in the sentence *He went to bed to take a __ap*, children use meaning clues to determine what word makes sense (*nap*) and what letter is needed to complete the word (*n*). Encourage children to use their prior knowledge and judgment skills to figure out what letters and words make sense.

◆ **Decoding:** Decoding takes place when children combine and synthesize a variety of reading skills (letter recognition, sound-letter relationships, and so on) in order to translate a printed word into a meaningful unit. The decoding activities in this book invite students to decipher 20 words and determine which ones are "real" (English-language) words and which are silly "nonsense" words. Before children begin, you may want to discuss how they can tell when a word is "real" (it has meaning and can be used in a sentence) and when it is "nonsense" (it has sounds, but no meaning).

◆ **Rhyming:** When children rhyme, they recognize and generate words that end with the same sound, such as *unfold* and *cold*. In this type of activity, children are given a target word and asked to generate three more words that end with the same target sound. For instance, when given the word *wag*, children might respond with the words *tag*, *bag*, and *rag*. Be sure to remind children that some words may rhyme without belonging to the same word family; for instance, *bite* rhymes with *sight*, but they belong to different families because the ending sounds are spelled differently.

◆ **Comprehending:** Children comprehend text when they gain meaning from written words. In this type of activity, children are asked to distinguish between sentences that make sense and those that are nonsense. Each sentence contains target phonograms from the packet, but only some have meaning. For instance, *I feel sad and mad* makes sense, while *I want to take a fat nap with the ham* does not. You might encourage children to use mental imagery (that is, create a picture in their minds that shows what the sentence is saying) in order to figure out whether it has real meaning.

◆ **Deducing:** When children deduce, they make inferences and reach a conclusion through logical reasoning. The deduction activities in this book encourage students to use their reasoning abilities to match an illustration to a short story. Children first read the story and then look at several pictures, only one of which matches the facts presented. Each story uses target phonograms from the packet. For instance, in the story "That Cat Fran!" children learn that *Fran is fat, does not have a bag, likes to eat jam*, and *is not sad*. They then need to eliminate the pictures of a skinny cat holding a bag, a skinny cat with a jar of jam, and a fat, sad cat in order to arrive at the picture of a fat, happy cat with a jar of jam. Before children try this type of activity, you might like to review comprehension skills, such as rereading for meaning and using the process of elimination.

◆ **Attending:** The attending activities in this book simply ask children to pay attention to how different words look. Spelling involves forming words by arranging letters in an accepted order, and the ability to spell depends on many skills, one of which is visual attention. In this type of activity, children are given a picture representing a target word along with three spelling choices, and are asked to choose the correct one. For instance, a picture of a postage stamp is grouped with the choices *stam, stapm,* and *stamp.* You might like to discuss strategies children can use to complete the activity, such as asking themselves, "Does this look right?" and consulting a dictionary if they're not sure.

Using the Lessons: Helpful Tips

Twenty Week-by-Week Word Family Packets is designed for maximum flexibility, so you can easily fit the activities into your curriculum and schedule, and tailor them to meet the individual needs of your classroom and students. Following are a few suggestions for making the program a perfect fit for your instructional needs.

Grouping Options

◆ **Independent Work:** You'll find that the activities in this book are not only lots of fun, but also easy for children to understand and complete on their own. You may want to model and review each type of activity throughout the first couple of packets, but since the same engaging activity formats are repeated throughout the book, children will likely be able to continue their word-family learning independently.

◆ **Partner Work:** Working with a partner can be beneficial for both struggling and advanced readers. When children at different levels work together, the less advanced child gets the help he or she needs, while the more advanced child gets the chance to articulate (and therefore reinforce) his or her thinking and problem-solving skills.

◆ **Small-Group Work:** Working collaboratively helps children gain a variety of word-attack skills, as they see how different students approach the same task. Of course, it's also terrific for building social skills!

◆ **Whole-Class Instruction:** The activities also lend themselves wonderfully to whole-group instruction. You might consider copying an activity sheet onto chart paper, so you can lead the class through the activity as children work with their individual copies. Another option is to copy a sheet onto a transparency and use it with an overhead projector.

Instructional Options

◆ **Complete Program:** You can lead children through the program packet by packet throughout the year, going at a pace that suits your schedule and children's skill levels. You may choose to do one packet a week, or use another time frame. You may decide to spend more time on some packets than on others, or to leave out certain packets or activities if you've covered those phonograms in another part of your curriculum. There are no hard-and-fast rules—the schedule is completely up to you!

◆ **Target Specific Phonograms:** You may find that children have mastered some word families but have trouble achieving automaticity with others. Simply select the activities that cover the specific phonograms that children need to practice.

◆ **Target Specific Reading Skills:** Remember, the activities are not only organized around phonograms, but also around core reading skills, such as deducing, attending, comprehending, and so on. If students need practice developing a core skill, simply group together the activities from each packet that cover the skill.

◆ **Target Specific Phonics Skills:** If you're teaching specific phonics skills, or have just completed a mini-lesson on a particular phonetic element, use the activity sheets to support your instruction. Simply choose the activities that address that element. For instance, if you've just done a lesson on the digraphs *sh* and *th*, you might choose the activity sheets that feature the phonograms *ush* and *oth*.

◆ **Homework Packets:** You can send the activity sheets home with children to do as independent homework assignments, or to encourage family involvement. Simply send a note home along with your chosen activities, explaining what children are learning by doing the exercises and encouraging caregivers to take time to work with children on the skills they're developing.

Scope and Sequence

Use the scope and sequence chart on page 13 to see at a glance the sounds, spelling patterns, and phonograms children will learn in each packet. The chart covers the 120 most essential word families; within this group, 35 of the most common phonograms are indicated in **bold**. You may want to place extra focus on these ending sounds, as they are the ones children are likely to encounter most often.

Week-by-Week Word Family Packets
Scope and Sequence Chart

PACKET	VOWEL SOUND AND SPELLING PATTERN	PHONOGRAMS
Packet 1	short *a*: cvc	**at**, ad, **ap**, ag, am, **an**
Packet 2	short *a*: cvcc	amp, and, ant, **ack**, **ash**, ask
Packet 3	short *i*: cvc	it, **in**, id, **ip**, ig, **ill**
Packet 4	short *i*: cvcc	int, ist, **ink**, **ing**, **ick**, ish
Packet 5	short *o*: cvc	ot, **op**, ox, og, ob, od
Packet 6	short *o*: cvcc	ond, ong, **ock**, oth, oss, ost
Packet 7	short *e*: cvc	et, en, ed, eg, ess, **ell**
Packet 8	short *e*: cvcc	end, elt, ent, **est**, eck, ench
Packet 9	short *u*: cvc	**ug**, um, un, us, up, ut
Packet 10	short *u*: cvcc	**ump**, ust, ush, **unk**, ung, **uck**
Packet 11	long *a*: cvce	**ake**, **ale**, **ame**, **ate**, ape, ave
Packet 12	important *a* exceptions	**ay**, **ain**, ail, **ank**, ang, eigh
Packet 13	long *o*: cvce	ope, **oke**, ove, one, ose, ole
Packet 14	important *o* exceptions	ow, oat, oad, old, o, oach
Packet 15	long *i*: cvce and exceptions	**ide**, **ice**, **ine**, **ight**, ite, y
Packet 16	long *e*: ee, ea	**eat**, each, eal, eep, eam, ee
Packet 17	long *u*: cvce and exceptions	ew, ue, ute, use, ool, oon
Packet 18	*r*-controlled vowels	ar, ark, irt, **ore**, orn, urt
Packet 19	diphthongs	out, ouch, ound, ouse, ow, own
Packet 20	broad *o*	**aw**, awl, awn, **all**, aught, ought

Name: _____

You will learn these word families:
at, ad, ap, ag, am, an

vowel + consonant

a + t ➡ cat

a + d ➡ dad

a + p ➡ map

a + g ➡ tag

a + m ➡ jam

a + n ➡ fan

Checklist
✔ off each page after you complete it.

✓ Activity 1

____ Activity 2

____ Activity 3

____ Activity 4

____ Activity 5

____ Activity 6

____ Activity 7

____ Activity 8

____ Activity 9

Name: _____

Which Words Live Here?

Use the letters and blends from the attic to make words in each word family. If you can't make any more real words, you can make nonsense words.

b c d f g h j k l

m n p r s t v w x y z br bl

ch cl cr dr fl fr gl gr kn pl pr sc scr

sh sk sl sm sn sp st str sw th thr tr wh wr

C at   b at   S at   m at   h at   Pr at

gl ad   br ad   cl ad   d ad   sk ad   b l ad

Pr ap   C ap   g ap   h ap   l ap   m ap

C ag   l ag   m ag   fl ag   b ag   C ag

b am   l am   pl am   W am   t am   C am

dr an   b an   ch an   m an   n an   l an

at, ad, ap, ag, am, an

Name: _____

Where Do You Hear It?

Do you hear the sound at the <u>B</u>EGINNING, <u>M</u>IDDLE, or <u>E</u>ND?
Circle the right answer.

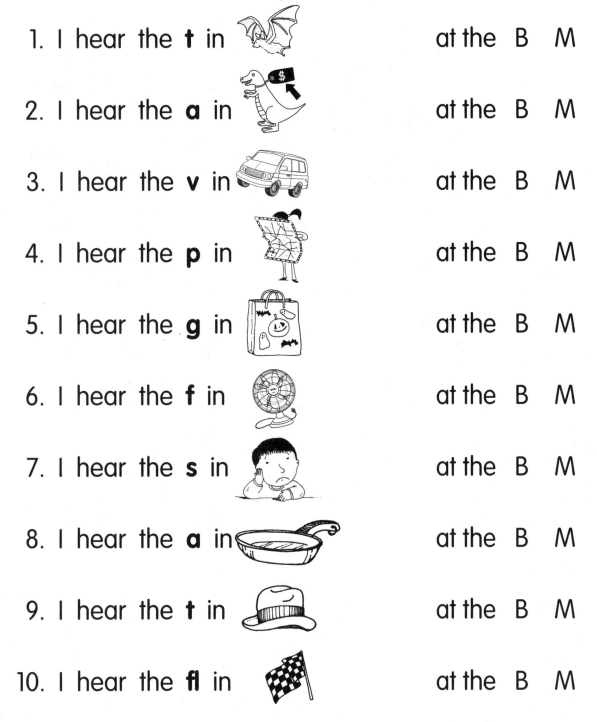

1. I hear the **t** in   at the   B   M   E

2. I hear the **a** in   at the   B   M   E

3. I hear the **v** in   at the   B   M   E

4. I hear the **p** in   at the   B   M   E

5. I hear the **g** in   at the   B   M   E

6. I hear the **f** in   at the   B   M   E

7. I hear the **s** in   at the   B   M   E

8. I hear the **a** in   at the   B   M   E

9. I hear the **t** in   at the   B   M   E

10. I hear the **fl** in   at the   B   M   E

at, ad, ap, ag, am, an

Name: _____

How Many Sounds Can You Hear?

Put your hand on top of the hand below. Read each of the words out loud SLOWLY. For every sound you hear, tap on a finger. How many taps were there? Circle that number.

an	2 3 4 5
bag	2 3 4 5
cap	2 3 4 5
mad	2 3 4 5
flat	2 3 4 5
cram	2 3 4 5
at	2 3 4 5
snaps	2 3 4 5
chap	2 3 4 5

at, ad, ap, ag, am, an

20 Week-by-Week Word Family Packets © 2008 by Lisa Fitzgerald McKeon, Scholastic Teaching Resources

Name: _____

Words From Earth or Mars?

Which words are real words we use on Earth? Which words are Martian words used only on Mars? Sort them.

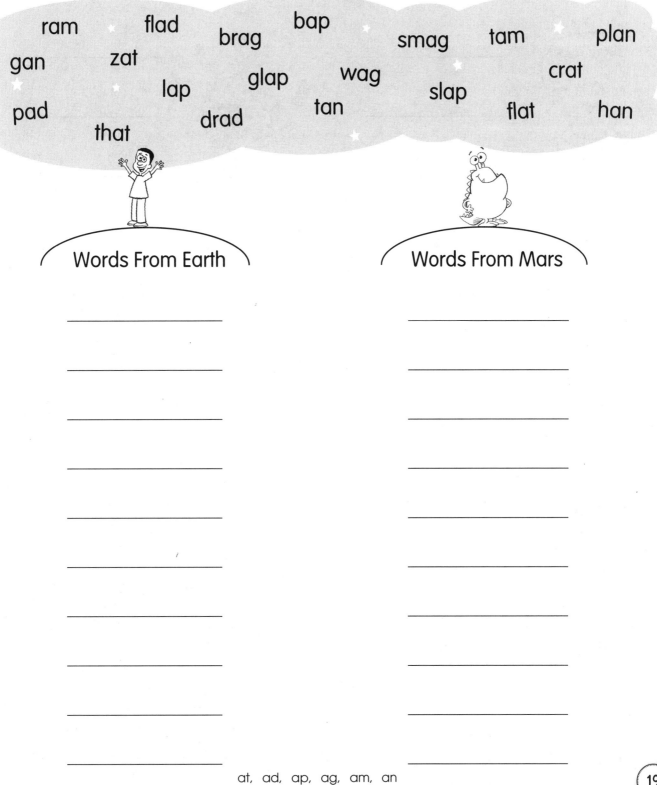

ram   flad   brag   bap   smag   tam   plan

gan   zat   glap   wag   crat

lap   slap

pad   tan   flat   han

that   drad

Words From Earth

_____

_____

_____

_____

_____

_____

_____

_____

Words From Mars

_____

_____

_____

_____

_____

_____

_____

_____

at, ad, ap, ag, am, an

They All Sound the Same

Can you think of three rhyming words to go with each picture?

mad
_____
_____
_____

wag
_____
_____
_____

cat
_____
_____
_____

ham
_____
_____
_____

map
_____
_____
_____

man
_____
_____
_____

at, ad, ap, ag, am, an

20 Week-by-Week Word Family Packets © 2008 by Lisa Fitzgerald McKeon, Scholastic Teaching Resources

Name: _____

What Is Missing?

Complete the sentences by using each of the letters and blends from the magnifying glass.

m   h
fl   v
c   n

1. My ____at says, "Meow."

2. My dad likes to eat ____am.

3. We can ride in the ____an.

4. The ____ag is red, white, and blue.

5. She made me so ____ad!

6. He went to bed to take a ____ap.

at, ad, ap, ag, am, an

Name: _____

Silly Sentences

Circle the silly sentences. For each silly sentence you find, color the shape with that number. What picture do you see?

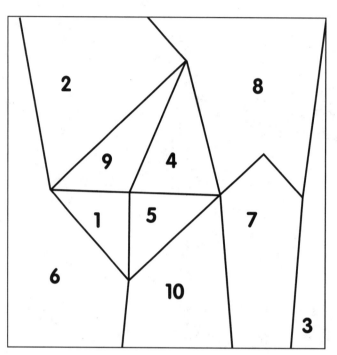

1. I want to take a fat nap with the ham.

2. I feel mad.

3. I can bat the ball.

4. I played tag with the rag and the pan.

5. That mad van looks like my dad.

6. I like to look at maps.

7. "Don't be sad," I said.

8. "You are a bad hat," said the sad flag.

9. That bag is a flat brat.

10. The cat sat by the man.

at, ad, ap, ag, am, an

20 Week-by-Week Word Family Packets © 2008 by Lisa Fitzgerald McKeon, Scholastic Teaching Resources

Name:

Read, Think, Then Read Again

Read the story below. Then color the picture that goes with it.

That Cat Fran!

Fran is fat.

Fran does <u>not</u> have a bag.

Fran likes to eat jam.

Fran is <u>not</u> sad.

at, ad, ap, ag, am, an

Name: _____

Which Spelling Is Right?

Look at each picture. Then circle the correct spelling of the word.

1. bat
   bart
   brat

4. glad
   lad
   gald

2. sap
   snat
   snap

5. flag
   lafg
   falg

3. clalm
   cam
   clam

6. van
   than
   fan

at, ad, ap, ag, am, an

Name: **Safiyyas**

vowel + consonant cluster

a + **mp** ➡ **lamp**

a + **nd** ➡ **hand**

a + **nt** ➡ **pants**

a + **ck** ➡ **backpack**

a + **sh** ➡ **crash**

a + **sk** ➡ **mask**

Checklist
✔ off each page after you complete it.

____ Activity 1

____ Activity 2

____ Activity 3

____ Activity 4

____ Activity 5

____ Activity 6

____ Activity 7

____ Activity 8

____ Activity 9

Name: _Safiyyas_

Which Words Live Here?

Use the letters and blends from the attic to make words in each word family. If you can't make any more real words, you can make nonsense words.

b c d f g h j k l

m n p r s t v w x y z br bl

ch cl cr dr fl fr gl gr kn pl pr sc scr

sh sk sl sm sn sp st str sw th thr tr wh wr

ch amp   L amp   SP amp   Str amp   Sw amp   Sc amp

C and   d and   Sl and   St and   Cl and   wl and

b ant   C ant   al ant   n ant   m ant   kn ant

g ack   fl ack   Sl ack   Sn ack   Sl ack   wk ack

lw ash   la ash   qw ash   w ash   Sw ash   kl ash

ch ask   nl ask   Cr ask   rl ask   lr ask   kl ask

amp, and, ant, ack, ash, ask

20 Week-by-Week Word Family Packets © 2008 by Lisa Fitzgerald McKeon, Scholastic Teaching Resources

Name: _Safiyyas_

Where Do You Hear It?

Do you hear the sound at the <u>B</u>EGINNING, <u>M</u>IDDLE, or <u>E</u>ND?
Circle the right answer.

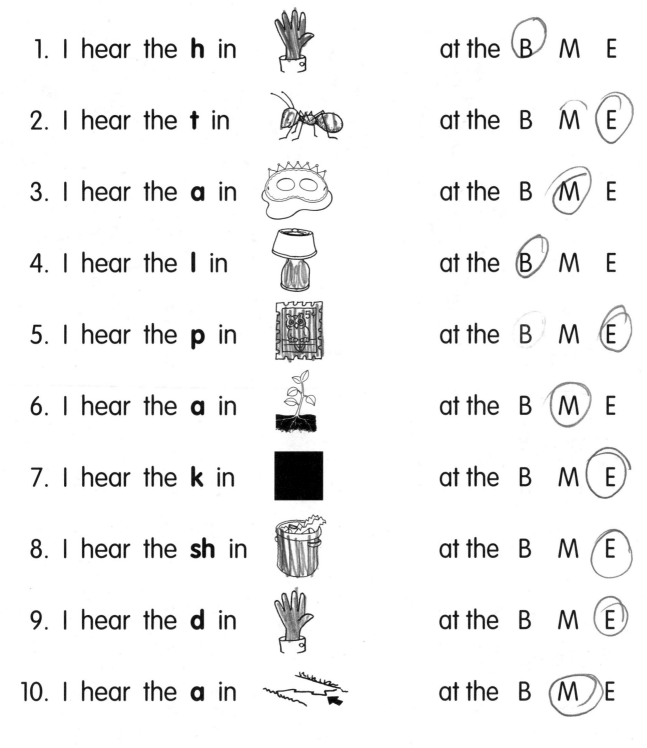

1. I hear the **h** in   at the Ⓑ M E

2. I hear the **t** in   at the B Ⓜ Ⓔ

3. I hear the **a** in   at the B Ⓜ E

4. I hear the **l** in   at the Ⓑ M E

5. I hear the **p** in   at the B M Ⓔ

6. I hear the **a** in   at the B Ⓜ E

7. I hear the **k** in   at the B M Ⓔ

8. I hear the **sh** in   at the B M Ⓔ

9. I hear the **d** in   at the B M Ⓔ

10. I hear the **a** in   at the B Ⓜ E

amp, and, ant, ack, ash, ask

Name: _____

How Many Sounds Can You Hear?

Put your hand on top of the hand below. Read each of the words out loud SLOWLY. For every sound you hear, tap on a finger. How many taps were there? Circle that number.

ask	2	3	4	5
champ	2	3	4	5
cap	2	3	4	5
quack	2	3	4	5
damp	2	3	4	5
bland	2	3	4	5
can't	2	3	4	5
ash	2	3	4	5
flask	2	3	4	5
land	2	3	4	5

amp, and, ant, ack, ash, ask

Name: _____

Words From Earth or Mars?

Which words are real words we use on Earth? Which words are Martian words used only on Mars? Sort them.

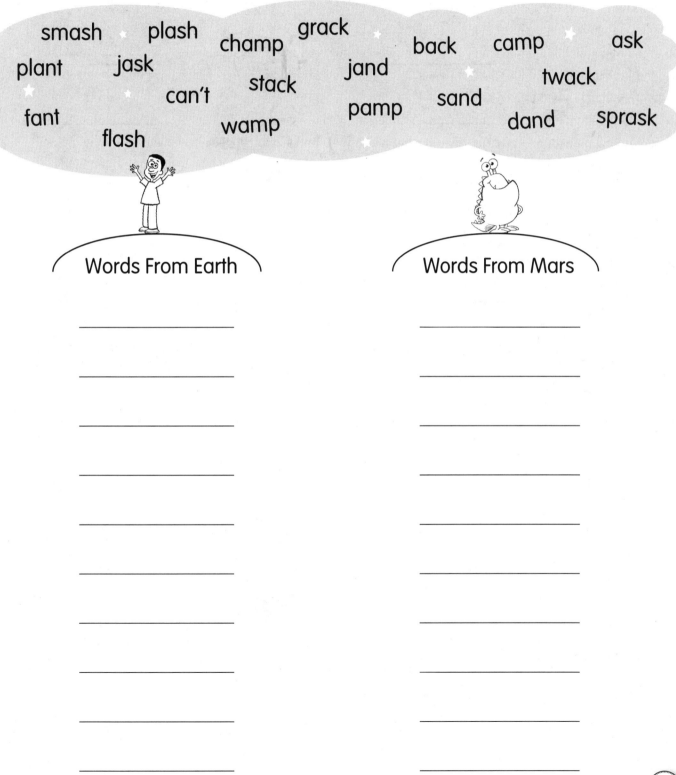

smash   plash   champ   grack   back   camp   ask
plant   jask   jand   twack
can't   stack   sand
fant   pamp   dand   sprask
flash   wamp

Words From Earth

Words From Mars

_____   _____

_____   _____

_____   _____

_____   _____

_____   _____

_____   _____

_____   _____

_____   _____

amp, and, ant, ack, ash, ask

Name: _____

They All Sound the Same

Can you think of three rhyming words to go with each picture?

crack _____
_____
_____

splash _____
_____
_____

hand _____
_____
_____

mask _____
_____
_____

lamp _____
_____
_____

plant _____
_____
_____

amp, and, ant, ack, ash, ask

20 Week-by-Week Word Family Packets © 2008 by Lisa Fitzgerald McKeon, Scholastic Teaching Resources

Name: _____

What Is Missing?

Complete the sentences by using each of the letters and blends from the magnifying glass.

st   sn

pl   r

m   h

1. She put a _____amp on the envelope.

2. Jack wore a _____ask on Halloween.

3. I have two _____ands and two feet.

4. The _____ant in my garden is growing very tall!

5. He loves to eat an apple at _____ack time.

6. Oh no, I have a red _____ash all over me!

amp, and, ant, ack, ash, ask

Name: _____

Silly Sentences

Circle the silly sentences. For each silly sentence you find, color the shape with that number. What picture do you see?

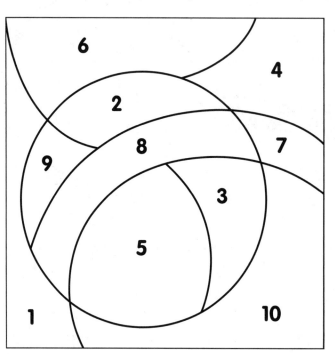

1. I made a big splash.

2. I love to eat sand, trash, and cash.

3. He likes to stand on top of his ant lamp.

4. I licked the stamp.

5. My pants said, "Quack!"

6. I will ask for a snack.

7. I said, "Give me my toy back!"

8. The plant had a task mask on.

9. I want to crack and smash the pants.

10. I like to go to camp.

amp, and, ant, ack, ash, ask

Name: _____

Read, Think, Then Read Again

Read the story below. Then color the picture that goes with it.

Jack and His Lamp

Jack Quack is <u>not</u> on land.

Jack Quack likes to read books by his lamp.

Jack Quack is <u>not</u> in a mask.

Jack Quack does <u>not</u> have a rash.

amp, and, ant, ack, ash, ask

Which Spelling Is Right?

Look at each picture. Then circle the correct spelling of the word.

1.

    stam

    stapm

    stamp

4.

    than

    hand

    thand

2.

    lant

    pland

    plant

5.

    crakc

    krack

    crack

3.

    cash

    kash

    cahs

6.

    ask

    mask

    maks

amp, and, ant, ack, ash, ask

Name: _____

You will learn these word families:
it, in, id, ip, ig, ill

vowel + consonant

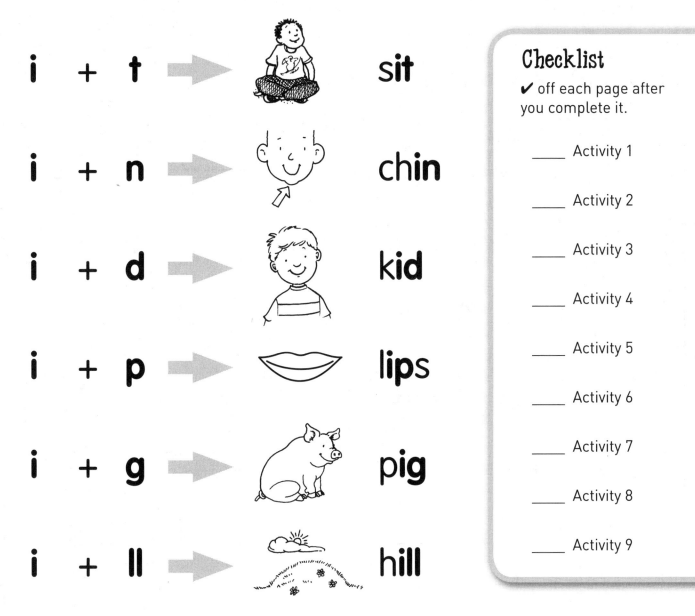

i + t → sit

i + n → chin

i + d → kid

i + p → lips

i + g → pig

i + ll → hill

Checklist
✔ off each page after you complete it.

_____ Activity 1

_____ Activity 2

_____ Activity 3

_____ Activity 4

_____ Activity 5

_____ Activity 6

_____ Activity 7

_____ Activity 8

_____ Activity 9

Name: _____

Which Words Live Here?

Use the letters and blends from the attic to make words in each word family. If you can't make any more real words, you can make nonsense words.

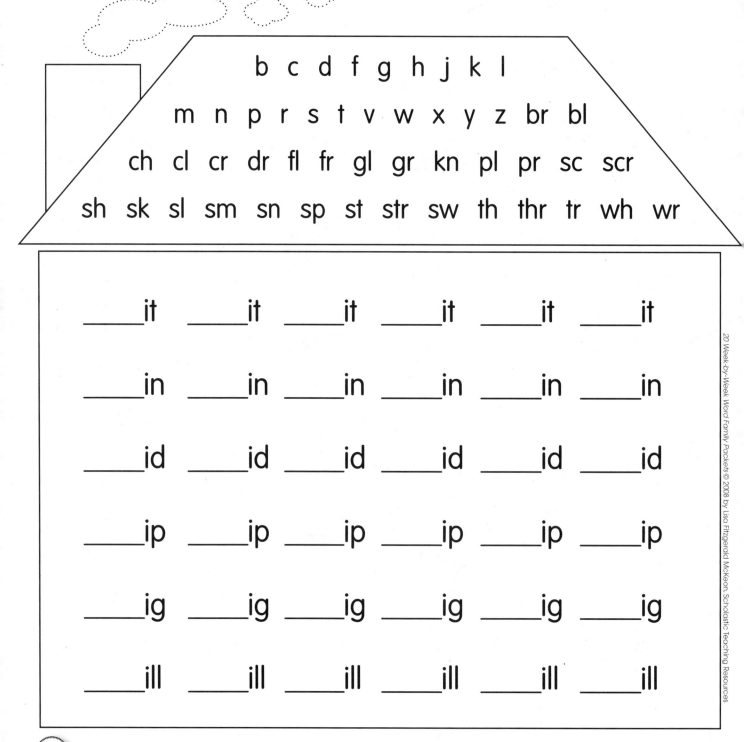

b c d f g h j k l

m n p r s t v w x y z br bl

ch cl cr dr fl fr gl gr kn pl pr sc scr

sh sk sl sm sn sp st str sw th thr tr wh wr

___it   ___it   ___it   ___it   ___it   ___it

___in   ___in   ___in   ___in   ___in   ___in

___id   ___id   ___id   ___id   ___id   ___id

___ip   ___ip   ___ip   ___ip   ___ip   ___ip

___ig   ___ig   ___ig   ___ig   ___ig   ___ig

___ill ___ill ___ill ___ill ___ill ___ill

it, in, id, ip, ig, ill

Name: _____

Where Do You Hear It?

Do you hear the sound at the <u>B</u>EGINNING, <u>M</u>IDDLE, or <u>E</u>ND?
Circle the right answer.

1. I hear the **p** in   at the   B   M   E

2. I hear the **i** in   at the   B   M   E

3. I hear the **p** in   at the   B   M   E

4. I hear the **l** in   at the   B   M   E

5. I hear the **i** in   at the   B   M   E

6. I hear the **sh** in   at the   B   M   E

7. I hear the **p** in   at the   B   M   E

8. I hear the **l** in   at the   B   M   E

9. I hear the **ch** in   at the   B   M   E

10. I hear the **t** in   at the   B   M   E

it, in, id, ip, ig, ill

Name: _____

How Many Sounds Can You Hear?

Put your hand on top of the hand below. Read each of the words out loud SLOWLY. For every sound you hear, tap on a finger. How many taps were there? Circle that number.

__quit__	2	3	4	5
__drip__	2	3	4	5
__still__	2	3	4	5
__big__	2	3	4	5
__did__	2	3	4	5
__split__	2	3	4	5
__ill__	2	3	4	5
__thrill__	2	3	4	5
__thin__	2	3	4	5

it, in, id, ip, ig, ill

20 Week-by-Week Word Family Packets © 2008 by Lisa Fitzgerald McKeon, Scholastic Teaching Resources

Name: _____

Words From Earth or Mars?

Which words are real words we use on Earth? Which words are
Martian words used only on Mars? Sort them.

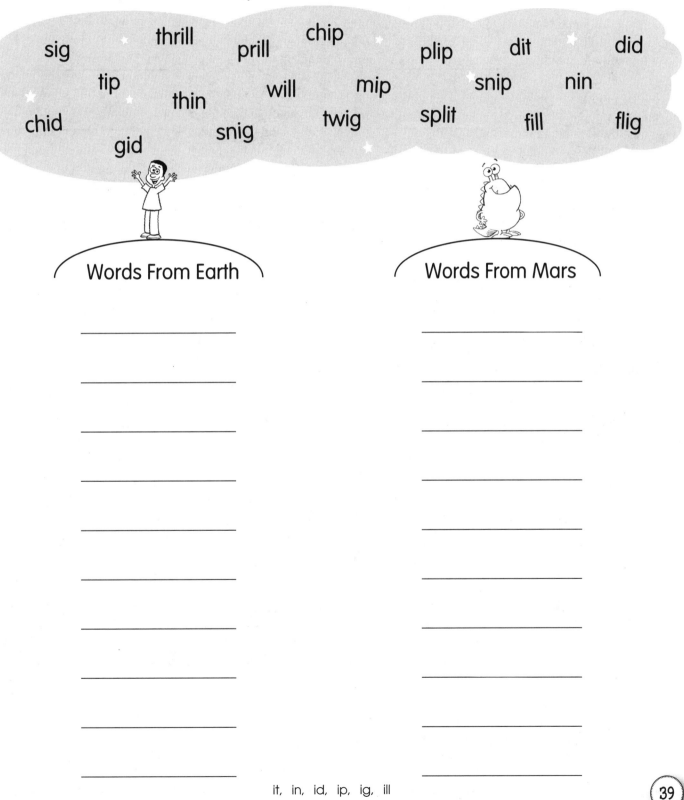

sig   thrill   prill   chip   plip   dit   did

tip   thin   will   mip   snip   nin

chid   snig   twig   split   fill   flig

gid

Words From Earth

Words From Mars

_____   _____

_____   _____

_____   _____

_____   _____

_____   _____

_____   _____

_____   _____

_____   _____

_____   _____

it, in, id, ip, ig, ill

Name: _____

They All Sound the Same

Can you think of three rhyming words to go with each picture?

sit _____
_____
_____

fin _____
_____
_____

ship _____
_____
_____

spill _____
_____
_____

dig _____
_____
_____

kid _____
_____
_____

it, in, id, ip, ig, ill

20 Week-by-Week Word Family Packets © 2008 by Lisa Fitzgerald McKeon, Scholastic Teaching Resources

Name: _____

What Is Missing?

Complete the sentences by using each of the letters and blends from the magnifying glass.

fl   l
b   sl
sp   ch

1. The baseball player ____id into home base.

2. He ____it the campfire.

3. Oops, I got food on my ____in!

4. We made a ____ig mess in the playroom!

5. I can do a ____ip all by myself!

6. I don't want to ____ill my drink!

it, in, id, ip, ig, ill

Name: _____

Silly Sentences

Circle the silly sentences. For each silly sentence you find, color the shape with that number. What picture do you see?

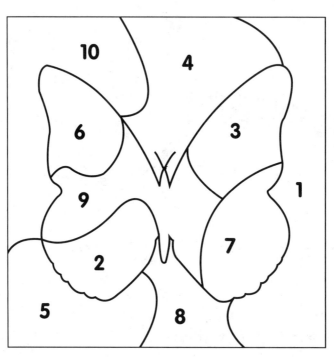

1. My brother was ill and had to sit down.

2. Dad said, "Let's dig a wig, kid."

3. The hill has a chin and lips.

4. My lips are red.

5. I ran fast and did not trip!

6. The grill did a jig and then quit.

7. I saw a shin spin with a big grin.

8. The kid hid in the big house.

9. The red pig will spill and hit and spit.

10. I have a twin sister.

it, in, id, ip, ig, ill

20 Week-by-Week Word Family Packets © 2008 by Lisa Fitzgerald McKeon, Scholastic Teaching Resources

Name: _____

Read, Think, Then Read Again

Read the story below. Then color the picture that goes with it.

Bill and Jill

Bill and Jill have grins.

They stand on a big hill.

Bill and Jill have twin pets.

The twin pets are pigs.

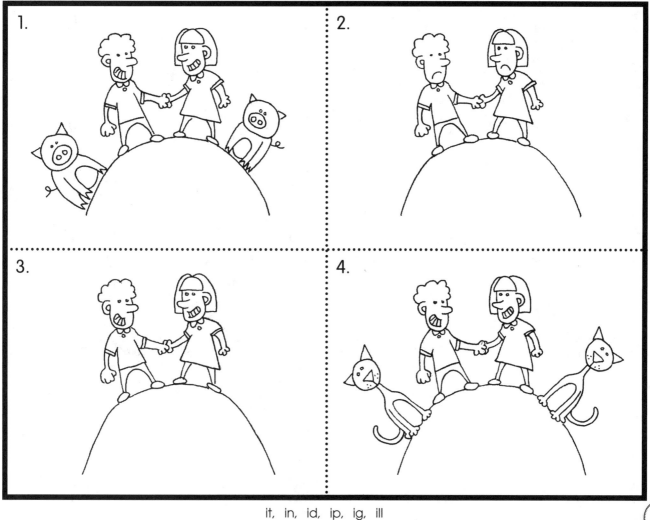

it, in, id, ip, ig, ill

Name: _____

Which Spelling Is Right?

Look at each picture. Then circle the correct spelling of the word.

1. pit

    plit

    pin

2. cid

    kid

    kidd

3   big

    dig

    digg

4. shin

    chin

    thin

5. drip

    dirp

    dip

6. spil

    slill

    spill

it, in, id, ip, ig, ill

Name: _____

You will learn these word families:
int, ist, ink, ing, ick, ish

vowel + consonant cluster

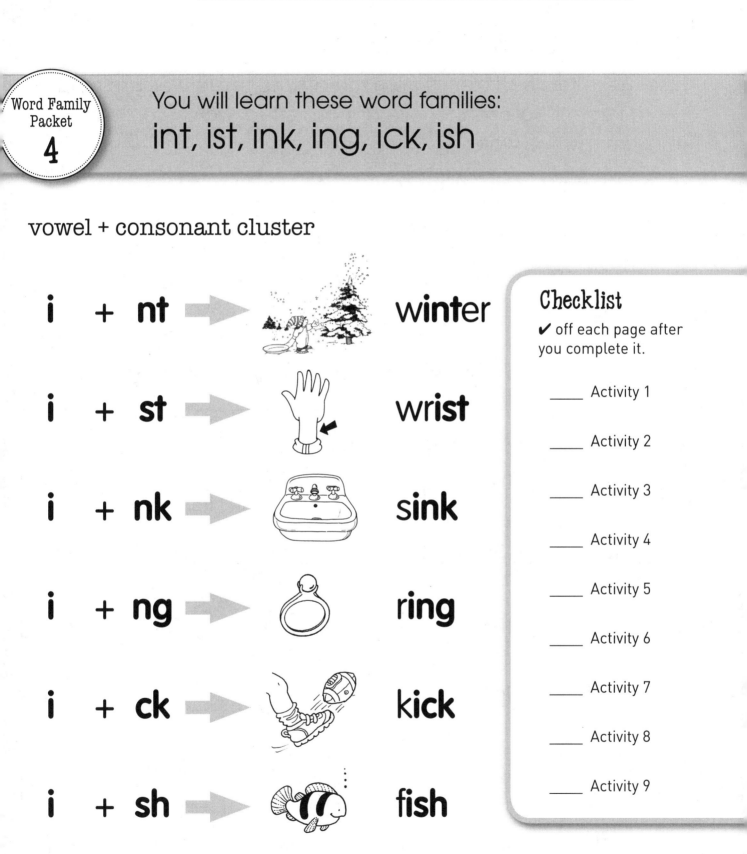

i + **nt** ➡ w**int**er

i + **st** ➡ wr**ist**

i + **nk** ➡ s**ink**

i + **ng** ➡ r**ing**

i + **ck** ➡ k**ick**

i + **sh** ➡ f**ish**

Checklist
✔ off each page after you complete it.

____ Activity 1

____ Activity 2

____ Activity 3

____ Activity 4

____ Activity 5

____ Activity 6

____ Activity 7

____ Activity 8

____ Activity 9

Name: _____

Which Words Live Here?

Use the letters and blends from the attic to make words in each word family. If you can't make any more real words, you can make nonsense words.

b c d f g h j k l

m n p r s t v w x y z br bl

ch cl cr dr fl fr gl gr kn pl pr sc scr

sh sk sl sm sn sp st str sw th thr tr wh wr

____int ____int ____int ____int ____int ____int

____ist ____ist ____ist ____ist ____ist ____ist

____ink ____ink ____ink ____ink ____ink ____ink

____ing ____ing ____ing ____ing ____ing ____ing

____ick ____ick ____ick ____ick ____ick ____ick

____ish ____ish ____ish ____ish ____ish ____ish

int, ist, ink, ing, ick, ish

Name: _____

Where Do You Hear It?

Do you hear the sound at the <u>B</u>EGINNING, <u>M</u>IDDLE, or <u>E</u>ND?
Circle the right answer.

1. I hear the **th** in   at the B   M   E

2. I hear the **g** in   at the B   M   E

3. I hear the **ch** in   at the B   M   E

4. I hear the **i** in   at the B   M   E

5. I hear the **r** in   at the B   M   E

6. I hear the **k** in   at the B   M   E

7. I hear the **k** in   at the B   M   E

8. I hear the **g** in   at the B   M   E

9. I hear the **i** in   at the B   M   E

10. I hear the **i** in   at the B   M   E

int, ist, ink, ing, ick, ish

Name: _____

How Many Sounds Can You Hear?

Put your hand on top of the hand below. Read each of the words out loud SLOWLY. For every sound you hear, tap on a finger. How many taps were there? Circle that number.

__hint__	2	3	4	5
__twist__	2	3	4	5
__wish__	2	3	4	5
__thick__	2	3	4	5
__wing__	2	3	4	5
__rink__	2	3	4	5
__chick__	2	3	4	5
__tick__	2	3	4	5
__list__	2	3	4	5

int, ist, ink, ing, ick, ish

Name: _____

Words From Earth or Mars?

Which words are real words we use on Earth? Which words are
Martian words used only on Mars? Sort them.

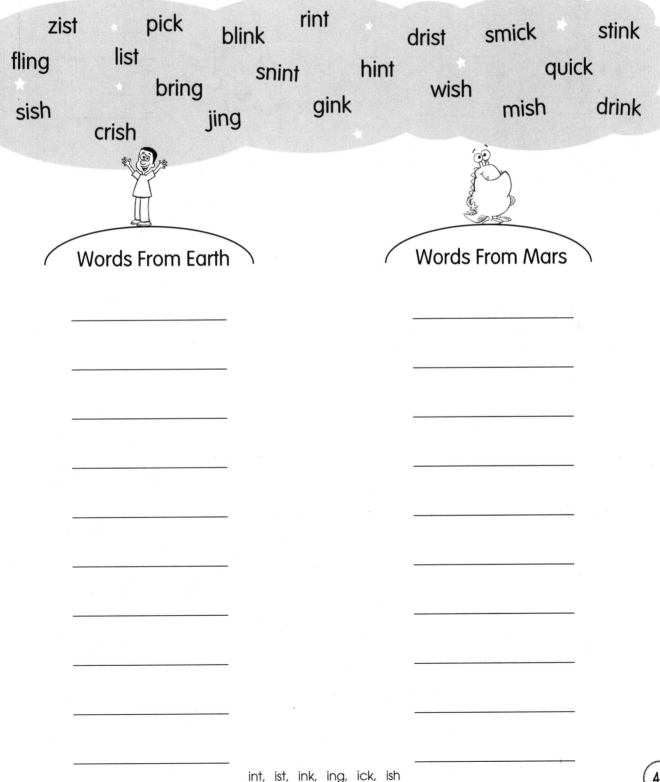

zist   pick   blink   rint   drist   smick   stink

fling   list   snint   hint   quick

bring   wish   stink

sish   gink   mish   drink

crish   jing

Words From Earth

Words From Mars

_____   _____

_____   _____

_____   _____

_____   _____

_____   _____

_____   _____

_____   _____

_____   _____

_____   _____

int, ist, ink, ing, ick, ish

Name: _____

They All Sound the Same

Can you think of three rhyming words to go with each picture?

sink _____

swing _____

fish _____

kick _____

wrist _____

sprint _____

int, ist, ink, ing, ick, ish

Name: _____

What Is Missing?

Complete the sentences by using each of the letters and blends from the magnifying glass.

sw   p

w   l

br   h

1. The teacher gave the boy a _____int.

2. Her favorite color is _____ink.

3. At school, I love to go on the _____ing .

4. One little pig had a _____ick house.

5. She made a birthday _____ish.

6. Mommy made us a shopping _____ist.

Name: _____

Silly Sentences

Circle the silly sentences. For each silly sentence you find, color the shape with that number. What picture do you see?

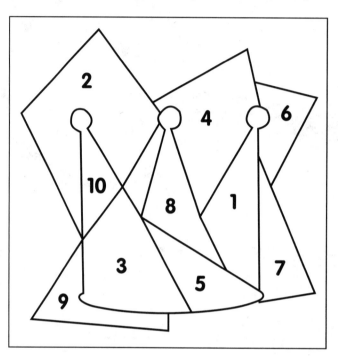

1. The pink ring wished for a fish.

2. I like to drink milk.

3. I am a big kick dish.

4. The chick is small.

5. She will king the sink.

6. I can blink and wink.

7. I like mint ice cream.

8. The chick is a brick.

9. Nick has a fish.

10. My ring can swing.

int, ist, ink, ing, ick, ish

20 Week-by-Week Word Family Packets © 2008 by Lisa Fitzgerald McKeon, Scholastic Teaching Resources

Read, Think, Then Read Again

Read the story below. Then color the picture that goes with it.

The King and the Ring

The king has a ring.

The king is <u>not</u> singing.

The king does <u>not</u> have anything on his wrists.

The king holds a chick.

int, ist, ink, ing, ick, ish

Name: _____

Which Spelling Is Right?

Look at each picture. Then circle the correct spelling of the word.

1. writs
   wrist
   rwist

4. drink
   drik
   dnirk

2. sing
   wing
   swing

5. sticz
   stikc
   sticks

3. fish
   fsh
   fihs

6. min
   nimt
   mint

int, ist, ink, ing, ick, ish

Name: _____

vowel + consonant

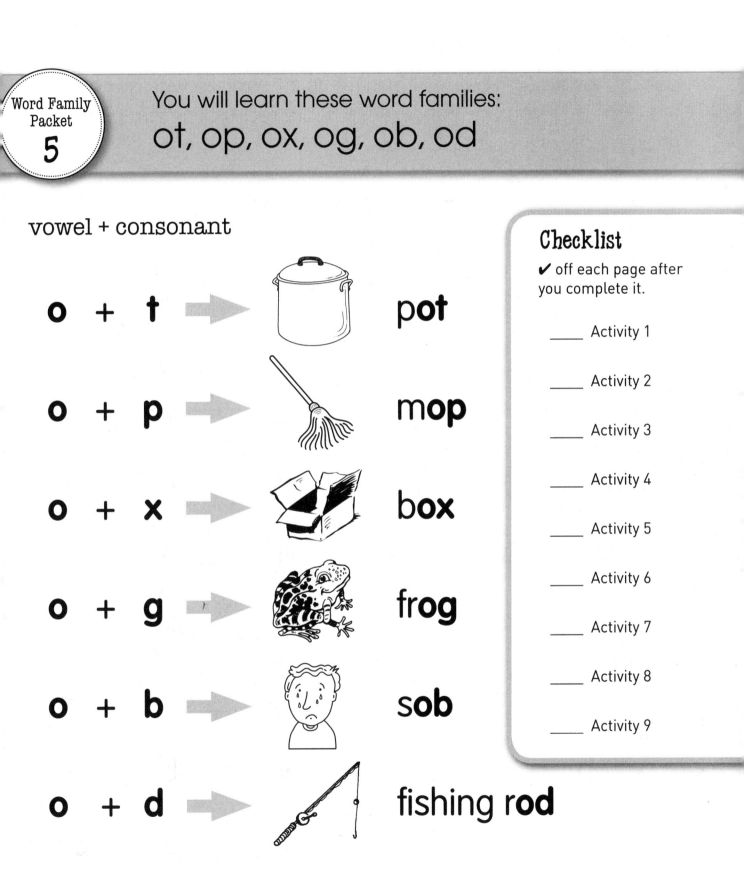

o + t ➡ **p**ot

o + p ➡ m**op**

o + x ➡ b**ox**

o + g ➡ fr**og**

o + b ➡ s**ob**

o + d ➡ fishing r**od**

Checklist
✔ off each page after you complete it.

_____ Activity 1

_____ Activity 2

_____ Activity 3

_____ Activity 4

_____ Activity 5

_____ Activity 6

_____ Activity 7

_____ Activity 8

_____ Activity 9

Name: _____

Which Words Live Here?

Use the letters and blends from the attic to make words in each word family. If you can't make any more real words, you can make nonsense words.

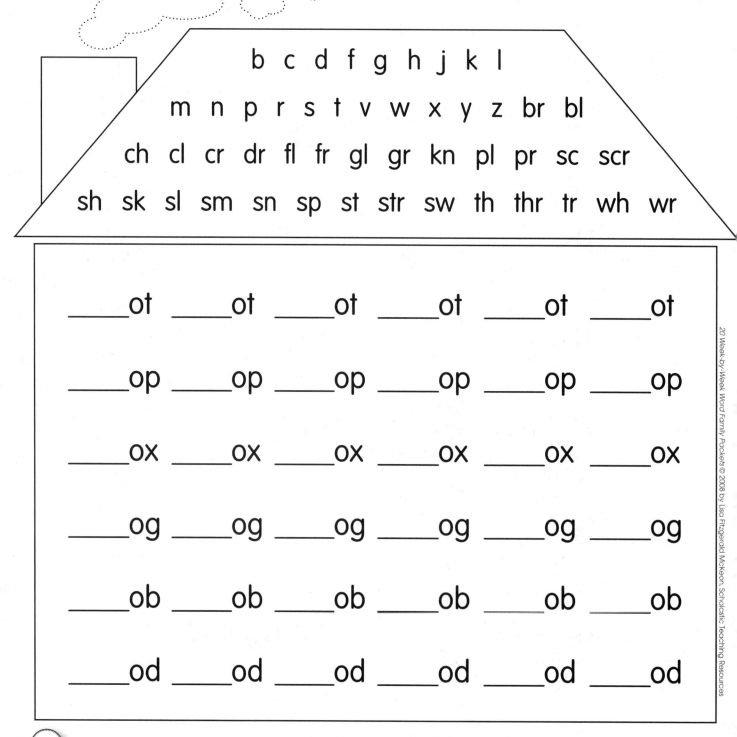

b c d f g h j k l

m n p r s t v w x y z br bl

ch cl cr dr fl fr gl gr kn pl pr sc scr

sh sk sl sm sn sp st str sw th thr tr wh wr

____ot ____ot ____ot ____ot ____ot ____ot

____op ____op ____op ____op ____op ____op

____ox ____ox ____ox ____ox ____ox ____ox

____og ____og ____og ____og ____og ____og

____ob ____ob ____ob ____ob ____ob ____ob

____od ____od ____od ____od ____od ____od

ot, op, ox, og, ob, od

Name: _____

Where Do You Hear It?

Do you hear the sound at the <u>B</u>EGINNING, <u>M</u>IDDLE, or <u>E</u>ND?
Circle the right answer.

1. I hear the **f** in   at the B   M   E

2. I hear the **b** in   at the B   M   E

3. I hear the **o** in   at the B   M   E

4. I hear the **r** in   at the B   M   E

5. I hear the **g** in   at the B   M   E

6. I hear the **x** in   at the B   M   E

7. I hear the **t** in   at the B   M   E

8. I hear the **sh** in   at the B   M   E

9. I hear the **o** in   at the B   M   E

10. I hear the **t** in   at the B   M   E

ot, op, ox, og, ob, od

Name: _____

How Many Sounds Can You Hear?

Put your hand on top of the hand below. Read each of the words out loud SLOWLY. For every sound you hear, tap on a finger. How many taps were there? Circle that number.

ox	2	3	4	5
pod	2	3	4	5
shop	2	3	4	5
spot	2	3	4	5
clog	2	3	4	5
throb	2	3	4	5
blot	2	3	4	5
box	2	3	4	5
robber	2	3	4	5

ot, op, ox, og, ob, od

20 Week-by-Week Word Family Packets © 2008 by Lisa Fitzgerald McKeon, Scholastic Teaching Resources

Name: _____

Words From Earth or Mars?

Which words are real words we use on Earth? Which words are Martian words used only on Mars? Sort them.

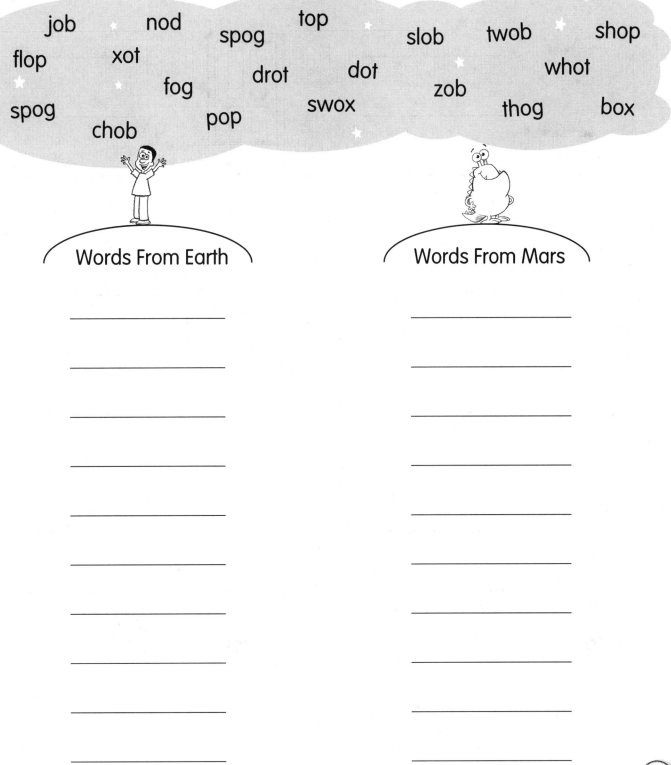

job   nod   spog   top   slob   twob   shop

flop   xot   drot   dot   whot

spog   fog   swox   zob   thog   box

chob   pop

Words From Earth

Words From Mars

_____   _____

_____   _____

_____   _____

_____   _____

_____   _____

_____   _____

_____   _____

_____   _____

ot, op, ox, og, ob, od

Name: _____

They All Sound the Same

Can you think of three rhyming words to go with each picture?

fox _____

knob _____

dog _____

rod _____

stop _____

knot _____

ot, op, ox, og, ob, od

20 Week-by-Week Word Family Packets © 2008 by Lisa Fitzgerald McKeon, Scholastic Teaching Resources

Name: _____

What Is Missing?

Complete the sentences by using each of the letters and blends from the magnifying glass.

j   c

f   sh

r   n

1. I love to eat corn on the ____ob.

2. I am ____ot going to the park.

3. Every morning my dad goes for a ____og.

4. I saw a ____ox in the woods.

5. I just got a brand new fishing ____od.

6. We had to make a stop at the pet ____op.

20 Week-by-Week Word Family Packets © 2008 by Lisa Fitzgerald McKeon, Scholastic Teaching Resources

Name: _____

Silly Sentences

Circle the silly sentences. For each silly sentence you find, color the shape with that number. What picture do you see?

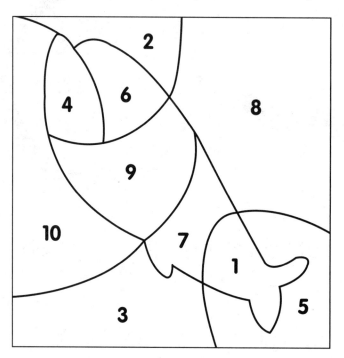

1. He got a lot of glob on his jog.

2. That pot is hot!

3. The fox lived in the woods.

4. No hog likes to jog in smog.

5. My mom hates to mop.

6. Oh no! My snob frog has a clog!

7. Flop the top and drop the pod rod.

8. My friend's mom got a job.

9. The ox ate the knob and robbed the spot hot.

10. My dad says that I am a slob.

ot, op, ox, og, ob, od

20 Week-by-Week Word Family Packets © 2008 by Lisa Fitzgerald McKeon, Scholastic Teaching Resources

Name: _____

Read, Think, Then Read Again

Read the story below. Then color the picture that goes with it.

Frog Shop

There are five frogs in the tank.

Three frogs do <u>not</u> have spots.

None of the frogs hop.

There is <u>not</u> a box in the tank.

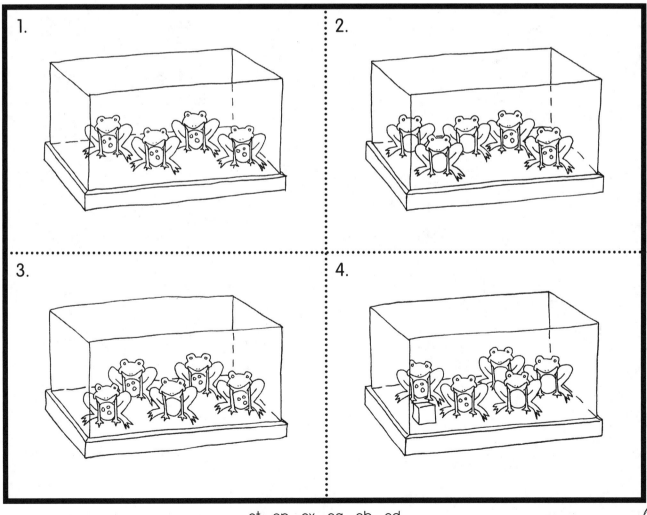

Name: _____

Which Spelling Is Right?

Look at each picture. Then circle the correct spelling of the word.

1. knot
   kot
   nokt

2. pox
   phox
   fox

3. rob
   robd
   rod

4. drob
   drop
   dorp

5. gog
   job
   jog

6. sod
   sox
   sob

64

ot, op, ox, og, ob, od

Word Family Packet 6

You will learn these word families:
ond, ong, ock, oth, oss, ost

vowel + consonant cluster

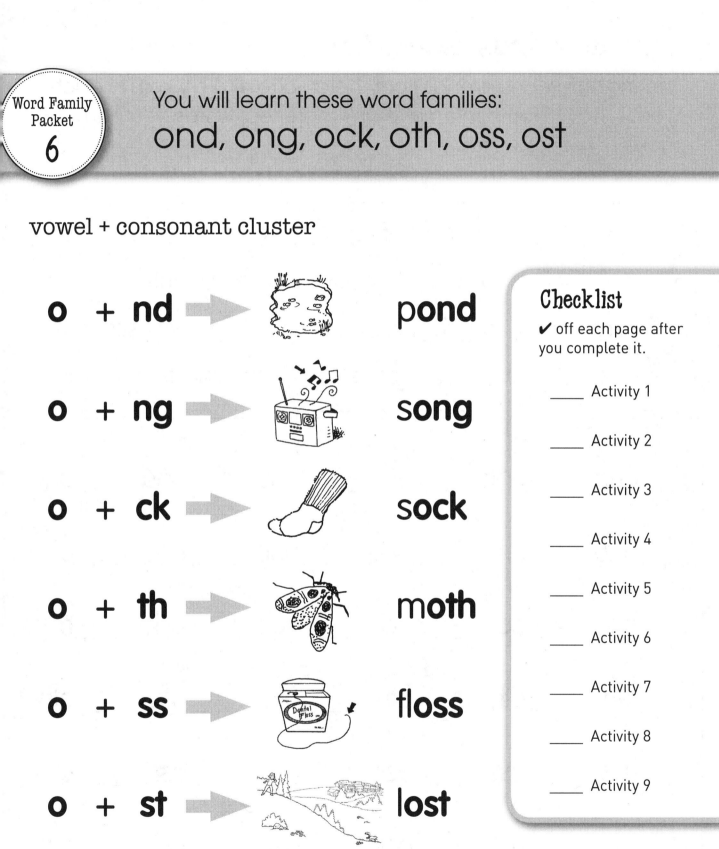

o + **nd** ➡ p**ond**

o + **ng** ➡ s**ong**

o + **ck** ➡ s**ock**

o + **th** ➡ m**oth**

o + **ss** ➡ fl**oss**

o + **st** ➡ l**ost**

Checklist
✔ off each page after you complete it.

____ Activity 1

____ Activity 2

____ Activity 3

____ Activity 4

____ Activity 5

____ Activity 6

____ Activity 7

____ Activity 8

____ Activity 9

Name: _____

Which Words Live Here?

Use the letters and blends from the attic to make words in each word family. If you can't make any more real words, you can make nonsense words.

b c d f g h j k l

m n p r s t v w x y z br bl

ch cl cr dr fl fr gl gr kn pl pr sc scr

sh sk sl sm sn sp st str sw th thr tr wh wr

____ond ____ond ____ond ____ond ____ond ____ond

____ong ____ong ____ong ____ong ____ong ____ong

____ock ____ock ____ock ____ock ____ock ____ock

____oth ____oth ____oth ____oth ____oth ____oth

____oss ____oss ____oss ____oss ____oss ____oss

____ost ____ost ____ost ____ost ____ost ____ost

ond, ong, ock, oth, oss, ost

20 Week-by-Week Word Family Packets © 2008 by Lisa Fitzgerald McKeon, Scholastic Teaching Resources

Name: _____

Where Do You Hear It?

Do you hear the sound at the <u>B</u>EGINNING, <u>M</u>IDDLE, or <u>E</u>ND?
Circle the right answer.

1. I hear the **p** in   at the   B   M   E

2. I hear the **th** in   at the   B   M   E

3. I hear the **s** in   at the   B   M   E

4. I hear the **o** in   at the   B   M   E

5. I hear the **fl** in   at the   B   M   E

6. I hear the **k** in   at the   B   M   E

7. I hear the **k** in   at the   B   M   E

8. I hear the **s** in   at the   B   M   E

9. I hear the **s** in   at the   B   M   E

10. I hear the **n** in   at the   B   M   E

ond, ong, ock, oth, oss, ost

Name: _____

How Many Sounds Can You Hear?

Put your hand on top of the hand below. Read each of the words out loud SLOWLY. For every sound you hear, tap on a finger. How many taps were there? Circle that number.

wrong	2	3	4	5
lock	2	3	4	5
fond	2	3	4	5
toss	2	3	4	5
clock	2	3	4	5
long	2	3	4	5
frost	2	3	4	5
moth	2	3	4	5
cloth	2	3	4	5

ond, ong, ock, oth, oss, ost

20 Week-by-Week Word Family Packets © 2008 by Lisa Fitzgerald McKeon, Scholastic Teaching Resources

Name: _____

Words From Earth or Mars?

Which words are real words we use on Earth? Which words are Martian words used only on Mars? Sort them.

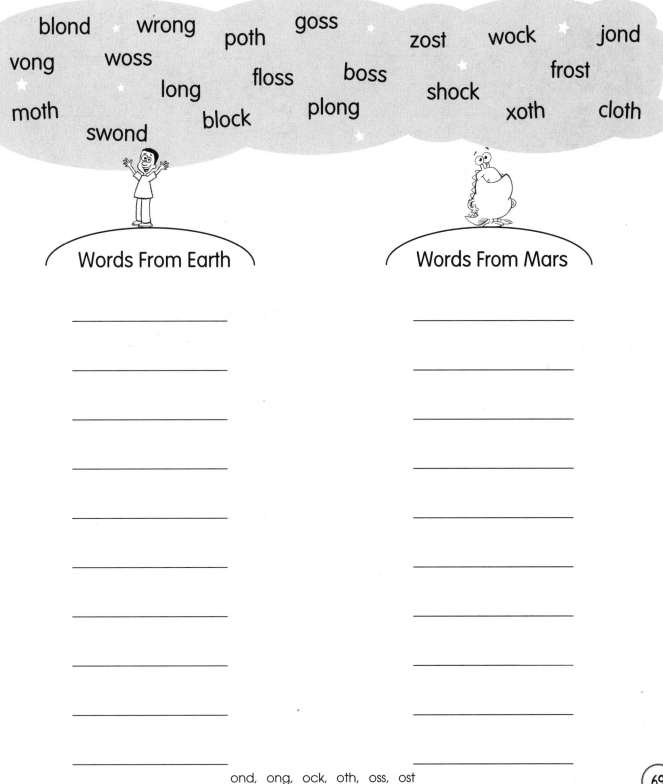

blond   wrong   poth   goss   zost   wock   jond

vong   woss   floss   boss   frost

long   shock

moth   plong   xoth   cloth

swond   block

Words From Earth

Words From Mars

_____

_____

_____

_____

_____

_____

_____

_____

_____

Name: _____

They All Sound the Same

Can you think of three rhyming words to go with each picture?

clock

_____
_____
_____

pond

_____
_____
_____

song

_____
_____
_____

floss

_____
_____
_____

frost

_____
_____
_____

cloth

_____
_____
_____

ond, ong, ock, oth, oss, ost

Name: _____

What Is Missing?

Complete the sentences by using each of the letters and blends from the magnifying glass.

fl   p

str   br

l   t

1. When I am sick my dad always gives me hot ____oth to sip.

2. He can lift 100 pounds! He is so ____ong.

3. Oh no, I ____ost my favorite sock!

4. I ____oss my teeth every night.

5. I like to fish with my brother at the ____ond

6. Tick ____ock goes my clock.

ond, ong, ock, oth, oss, ost

Name: _____

Silly Sentences

Circle the silly sentences. For each silly sentence you find, color the shape with that number. What picture do you see?

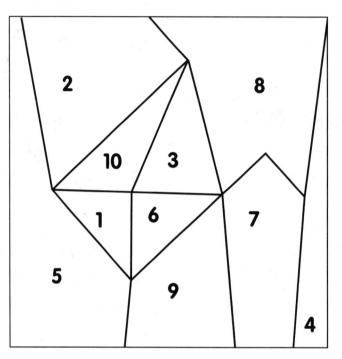

1. Dong bong went the sock.

2. I swam in the pond.

3. The strong song is made of floss.

4. You are wrong!

5. In the old days, a dress was called a frock.

6. The cloth is fond of moss.

7. Today, my sister is the boss.

8. I like to have hot socks in my broth.

9. I lost my sock.

10. The smock was blond and locked.

ond, ong, ock, oth, oss, ost

Name: _____

Read, Think, Then Read Again

Read the story below. Then color the picture that goes with it.

The House on the Block

The house has six long windows.

There are two big rocks near the car.

There are socks hanging outside.

There is <u>not</u> a pond.

ond, ong, ock, oth, oss, ost

Name: _____

Which Spelling Is Right?

Look at each picture. Then circle the correct spelling of the word.

1. plond

   prond

   pond

2. cloc

   clokc

   clock

3. toss

   tos

   tross

4. song

   strong

   sronge

5. moth

   mot

   moh

6. fwost

   forst

   frost

ond, ong, ock, oth, oss, ost

Name: _____

You will learn these word families:
et, en, ed, eg, ess, ell

vowel + consonant

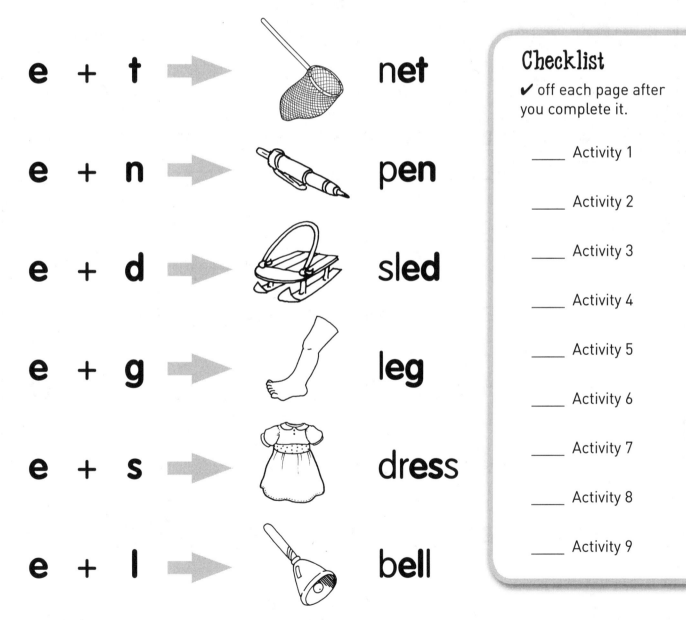

e + t ➡ net

e + n ➡ pen

e + d ➡ sled

e + g ➡ leg

e + s ➡ dress

e + l ➡ bell

Checklist
✔ off each page after you complete it.

____ Activity 1

____ Activity 2

____ Activity 3

____ Activity 4

____ Activity 5

____ Activity 6

____ Activity 7

____ Activity 8

____ Activity 9

Name: _____

Which Words Live Here?

Use the letters and blends from the attic to make words in each word family. If you can't make any more real words, you can make nonsense words.

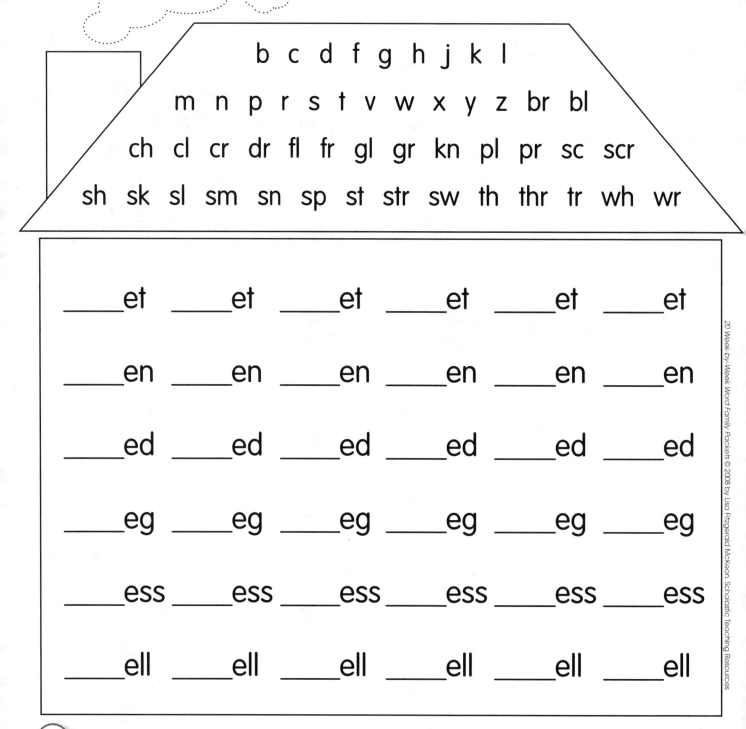

b c d f g h j k l

m n p r s t v w x y z br bl

ch cl cr dr fl fr gl gr kn pl pr sc scr

sh sk sl sm sn sp st str sw th thr tr wh wr

____et ____et ____et ____et ____et ____et

____en ____en ____en ____en ____en ____en

____ed ____ed ____ed ____ed ____ed ____ed

____eg ____eg ____eg ____eg ____eg ____eg

____ess ____ess ____ess ____ess ____ess ____ess

____ell ____ell ____ell ____ell ____ell ____ell

et, en, ed, eg, ess, ell

20 Week-by-Week Word Family Packets © 2008 by Lisa Fitzgerald McKeon, Scholastic Teaching Resources

Name: _____

Where Do You Hear It?

Do you hear the sound at the <u>B</u>EGINNING, <u>M</u>IDDLE, or <u>E</u>ND?
Circle the right answer.

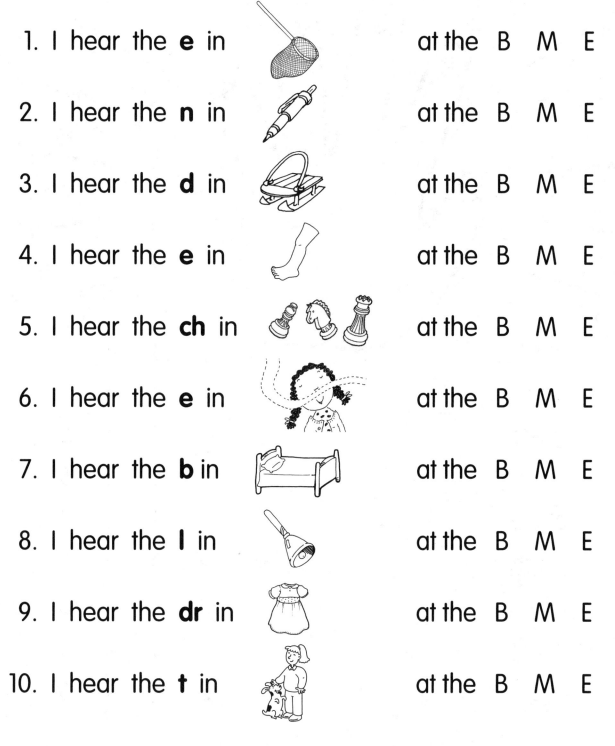

1. I hear the **e** in   at the   B   M   E

2. I hear the **n** in   at the   B   M   E

3. I hear the **d** in   at the   B   M   E

4. I hear the **e** in   at the   B   M   E

5. I hear the **ch** in   at the   B   M   E

6. I hear the **e** in   at the   B   M   E

7. I hear the **b** in   at the   B   M   E

8. I hear the **l** in   at the   B   M   E

9. I hear the **dr** in   at the   B   M   E

10. I hear the **t** in   at the   B   M   E

et, en, ed, eg, ess, ell

Name: _____

How Many Sounds Can You Hear?

Put your hand on top of the hand below. Read each of the
words out loud SLOWLY. For every sound you hear, tap on a finger.
How many taps were there? Circle that number.

wet	2	3	4	5
sled	2	3	4	5
chess	2	3	4	5
beg	2	3	4	5
shed	2	3	4	5
shred	2	3	4	5
when	2	3	4	5
swell	2	3	4	5
yet	2	3	4	5

et, en, ed, eg, ess, ell

20 Week-by-Week Word Family Packets © 2008 by Lisa Fitzgerald McKeon, Scholastic Teaching Resources

Name: _____

Words From Earth or Mars?

Which words are real words we use on Earth? Which words are Martian words used only on Mars? Sort them.

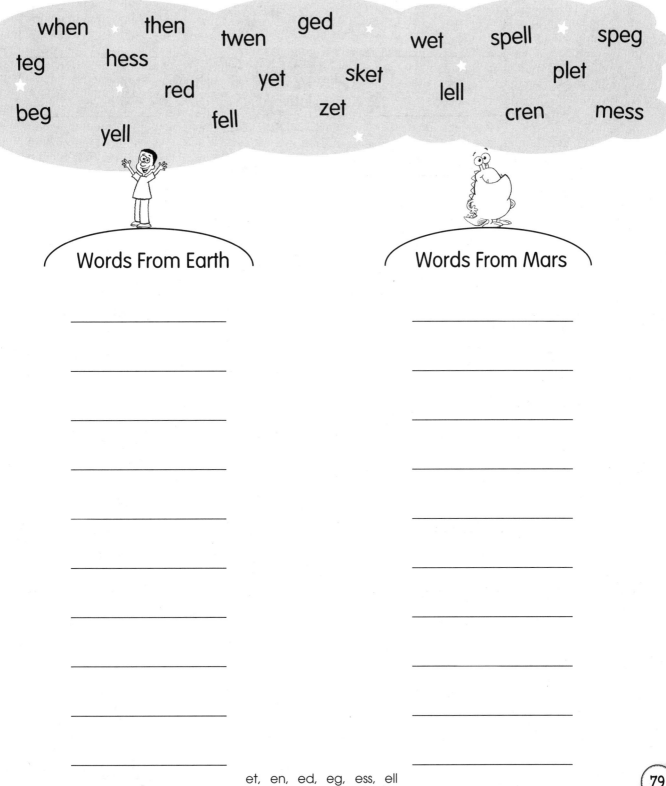

when   then   twen   ged   wet   spell   speg

teg   hess   sket   plet

red   yet   lell   cren   mess

beg   fell   zet

yell

Words From Earth

Words From Mars

_____   _____

_____   _____

_____   _____

_____   _____

_____   _____

_____   _____

_____   _____

_____   _____

_____   _____

et, en, ed, eg, ess, ell

Name: _____

They All Sound the Same

Can you think of three rhyming words to go with each picture?

shell _____

ten _____

bed _____

leg _____

dress _____

wet _____

20 Week-by-Week Word Family Packets © 2008 by Lisa Fitzgerald McKeon, Scholastic Teaching Resources

et, en, ed, eg, ess, ell

Name: _____

What Is Missing?

Complete the sentences by using each of the letters and blends from the magnifying glass.

b   sp

m   p

l   t

1. We made a big ____ess in the playroom.

2. I love to ____et my dog.

3. Do not jump on the ____ed.

4. I know how to ____ell lots of words.

5. Ow! I hurt my ____eg!

6. ____en apples fell off the tree.

et, en, ed, eg, ess, ell

Name: _____

Silly Sentences

Circle the silly sentences. For each silly sentence you find, color the shape with that number. What picture do you see?

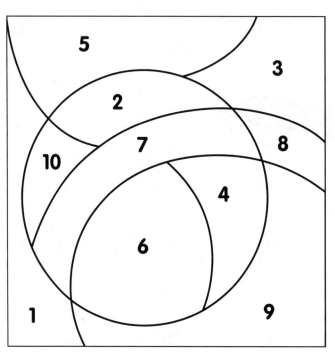

1. The red hen made a mess.

2. The sled wed Ted.

3. Fred went on his sled.

4. The wet bell has legs.

5. I love to play chess.

6. When you yell, I smell a shell!

7. Ben fed the hen ten nets and two sheds.

8. I bought a shell and a bell.

9. The toy jet was red.

10. The pets wore red net dresses and jets.

et, en, ed, eg, ess, ell

20 Week-by-Week Word Family Packets © 2008 by Lisa Fitzgerald McKeon, Scholastic Teaching Resources

Name: _____

Read, Think, Then Read Again

Read the story below. Then color the picture that goes with it.

Ben's Pet

Ben's pet has four legs.

There is a bell on his pet's neck.

His pet's name is Fred.

Ben does <u>not</u> have a pet dog.

1.

2.

3.

4.

et, en, ed, eg, ess, ell

Name: _____

Which Spelling Is Right?

Look at each picture. Then circle the correct spelling of the word.

1. upet

   upst

   upset

2. hed

   ched

   shed

3. drese

   drest

   dress

4. pren

   pen

   plen

5. legg

   leeg

   leg

6. smele

   smell

   small

et, en, ed, eg, ess, ell

Name: _____

You will learn these word families:
end, elt, ent, est, eck, ench

vowel + consonant cluster

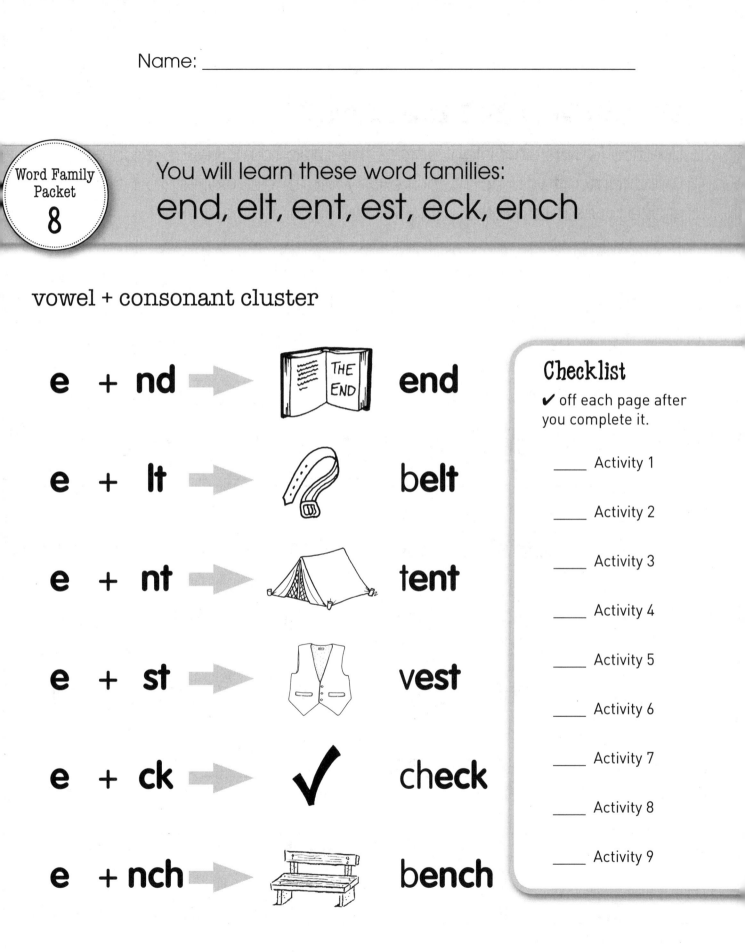

e + nd ➡ end

e + lt ➡ belt

e + nt ➡ tent

e + st ➡ vest

e + ck ➡ check

e + nch ➡ bench

Checklist
✔ off each page after you complete it.

_____ Activity 1

_____ Activity 2

_____ Activity 3

_____ Activity 4

_____ Activity 5

_____ Activity 6

_____ Activity 7

_____ Activity 8

_____ Activity 9

Name: _____

Which Words Live Here?

Use the letters and blends from the attic to make words in each word family. If you can't make any more real words, you can make nonsense words.

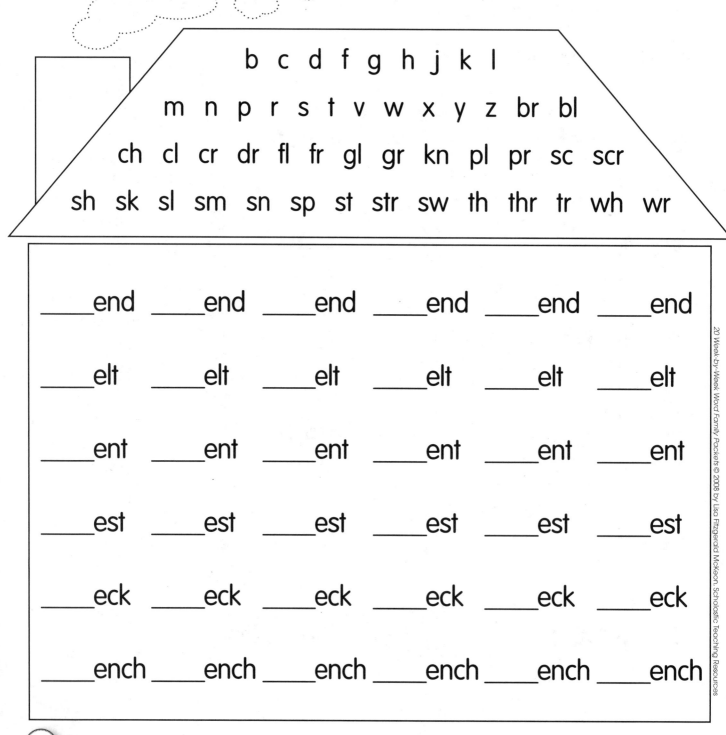

b c d f g h j k l

m n p r s t v w x y z br bl

ch cl cr dr fl fr gl gr kn pl pr sc scr

sh sk sl sm sn sp st str sw th thr tr wh wr

____end ____end ____end ____end ____end ____end

____elt ____elt ____elt ____elt ____elt ____elt

____ent ____ent ____ent ____ent ____ent ____ent

____est ____est ____est ____est ____est ____est

____eck ____eck ____eck ____eck ____eck ____eck

____ench ____ench ____ench ____ench ____ench ____ench

end, elt, ent, est, eck, ench

20 Week-by-Week Word Family Packets © 2008 by Lisa Fitzgerald McKeon, Scholastic Teaching Resources

Name: _____

Where Do You Hear It?

Do you hear the sound at the BEGINNING, MIDDLE, or END?
Circle the right answer.

1. I hear the **k** in   at the B M E

2. I hear the **ch** in   at the B M E

3. I hear the **n** in   at the B M E

4. I hear the **b** in   at the B M E

5. I hear the **e** in   at the B M E

6. I hear the **m** in   at the B M E

7. I hear the **n** in   at the B M E

8. I hear the **v** in   at the B M E

9. I hear the **e** in   at the B M E

10. I hear the **ch** in   at the B M E

end, elt, ent, est, eck, ench

Name: _____

How Many Sounds Can You Hear?

Put your hand on top of the hand below. Read each of the words out loud SLOWLY. For every sound you hear, tap on a finger. How many taps were there? Circle that number.

__end__	2	3	4	5
__wrench__	2	3	4	5
__dent__	2	3	4	5
__felt__	2	3	4	5
__check__	2	3	4	5
__best__	2	3	4	5
__sent__	2	3	4	5
__tend__	2	3	4	5
__quench__	2	3	4	5

end, elt, ent, est, eck, ench

20 Week-by-Week Word Family Packets © 2008 by Lisa Fitzgerald McKeon, Scholastic Teaching Resources

Name: _____

Words From Earth or Mars?

Which words are real words we use on Earth? Which words are Martian words used only on Mars? Sort them.

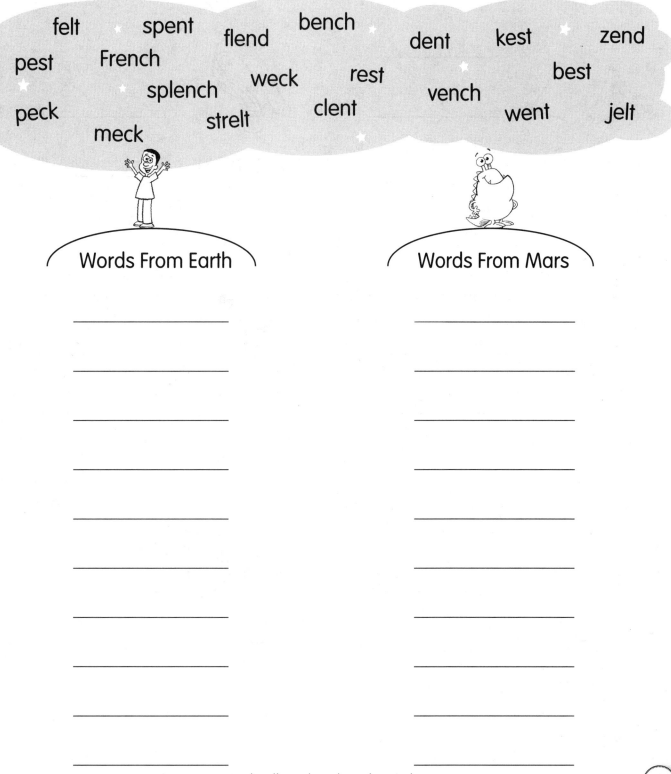

felt   spent   bench   dent   kest   zend

flend

pest   French   weck   rest   best

splench   vench

peck   clent   went   jelt

strelt

meck

Words From Earth

Words From Mars

_____   _____

_____   _____

_____   _____

_____   _____

_____   _____

_____   _____

_____   _____

_____   _____

_____   _____

end, elt, ent, est, eck, ench

Name: _____

They All Sound the Same

Can you think of three rhyming words to go with each picture?

tent

belt

vest

check

bench

end

end, elt, ent, est, eck, ench

Name: _____

What Is Missing?

Complete the sentences by using each of the letters and blends from the magnifying glass.

b   s

wr   f

l   n

1. My dad ____ent my mom flowers.

2. I put the hammer and ____ench in the toolbox.

3. Can you ____end me a hand?

4. She ____elt sick.

5. I always try my ____est!

6. A bug bit me on the ____eck.

end, elt, ent, est, eck, ench

Name: _____

Silly Sentences

Circle the silly sentences. For each silly sentence you find, color the shape with that number. What picture do you see?

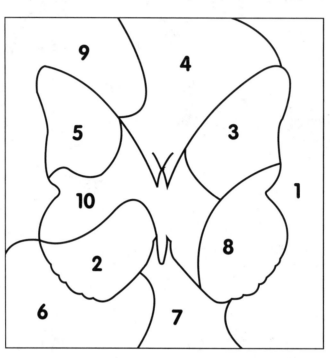

1. You were the best guest at the party!

2. The vest went west for the wrench test.

3. The bent check melted.

4. She sent her friend a gift.

5. The best pest felt like a felt welt.

6. He bent down when he felt dizzy.

7. I don't want my birthday to end!

8. The zest had the best stench.

9. He spent every cent that he had.

10. The fleck had one heck of a speck.

end, elt, ent, est, eck, ench

20 Week-by-Week Word Family Packets © 2008 by Lisa Fitzgerald McKeon, Scholastic Teaching Resources

Name: _____

Read, Think, Then Read Again

Read the story below. Then color the picture that goes with it.

The Bench

Two girls are sitting on the bench to take a rest.

One girl has a vest on.

A boy is standing next to the bench.

There is <u>not</u> a tent by the bench.

1.

2.

3.

4.

end, elt, ent, est, eck, ench

Name: _____

Which Spelling Is Right?

Look at each picture. Then circle the correct spelling of the word.

1. blendr
   bend
   blend

2. drent
   den
   dent

3. chekc
   jeck
   check

4. blt
   bellt
   belt

5. chets
   jest
   chest

6. bnch
   bench
   benck

end, elt, ent, est, eck, ench

Name: _____

vowel + consonant

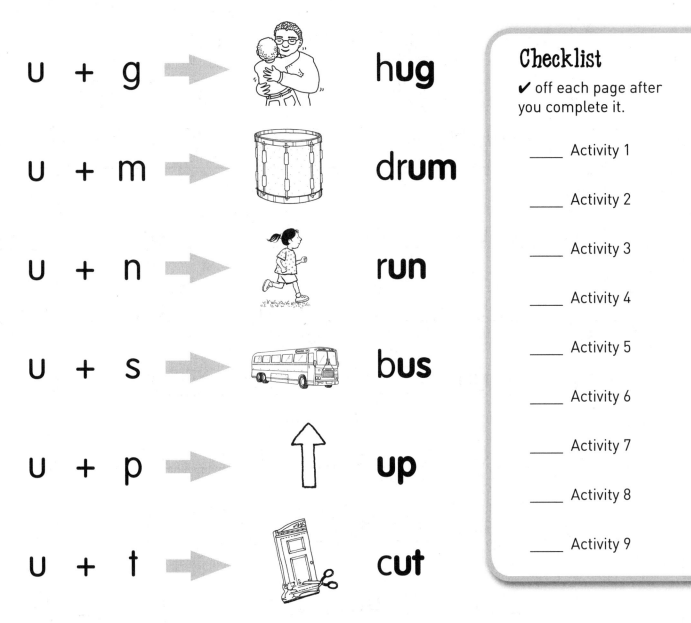

u + g ➡ h**ug**

u + m ➡ dr**um**

u + n ➡ r**un**

u + s ➡ b**us**

u + p ➡ **up**

u + t ➡ c**ut**

Checklist
✔ off each page after you complete it.

_____ Activity 1

_____ Activity 2

_____ Activity 3

_____ Activity 4

_____ Activity 5

_____ Activity 6

_____ Activity 7

_____ Activity 8

_____ Activity 9

Name: _____

Which Words Live Here?

Use the letters and blends from the attic to make words in each word family. If you can't make any more real words, you can make nonsense words.

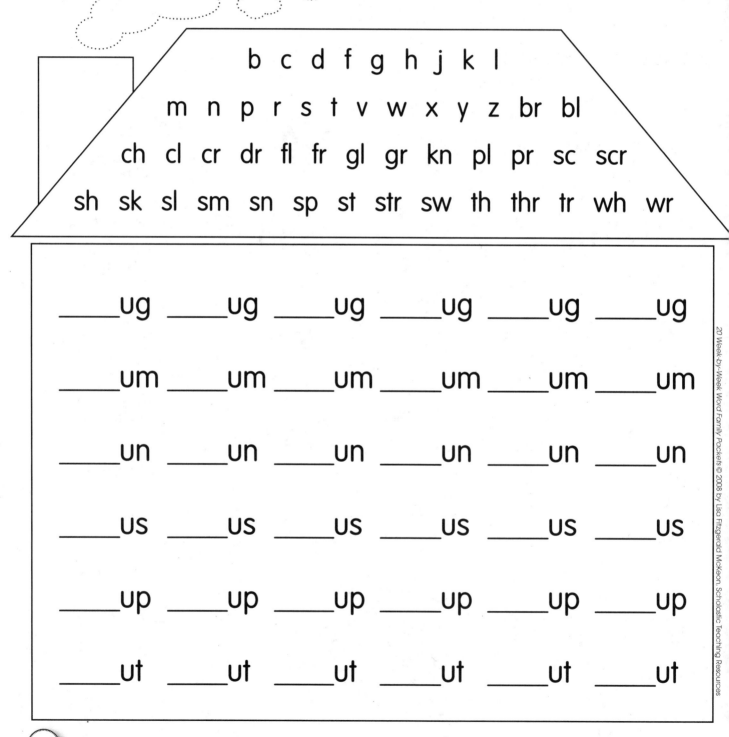

b c d f g h j k l

m n p r s t v w x y z br bl

ch cl cr dr fl fr gl gr kn pl pr sc scr

sh sk sl sm sn sp st str sw th thr tr wh wr

____ug ____ug ____ug ____ug ____ug ____ug

____um ____um ____um ____um ____um ____um

____un ____un ____un ____un ____un ____un

____us ____us ____us ____us ____us ____us

____up ____up ____up ____up ____up ____up

____ut ____ut ____ut ____ut ____ut ____ut

ug, um, un, us, up, ut

20 Week-by-Week Word Family Packets © 2008 by Lisa Fitzgerald McKeon, Scholastic Teaching Resources

Name: _____

Where Do You Hear It?

Do you hear the sound at the BEGINNING, MIDDLE, or END?
Circle the right answer.

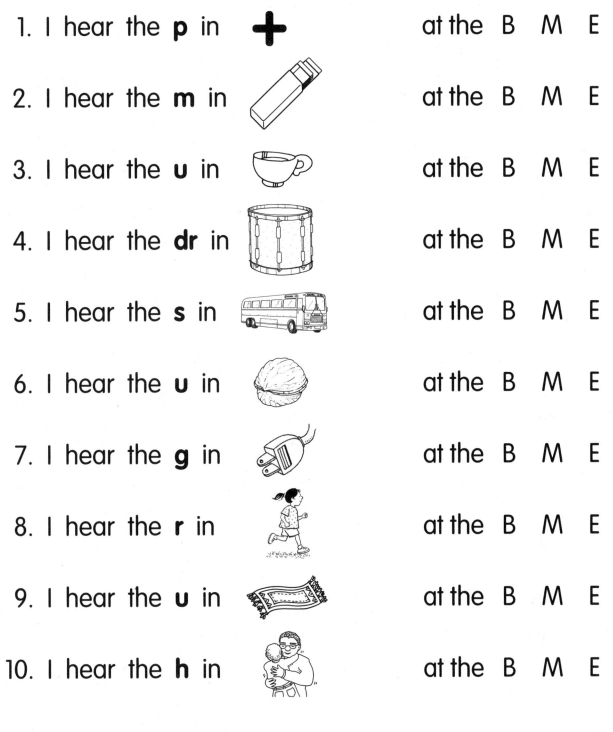

1. I hear the **p** in   at the   B   M   E

2. I hear the **m** in   at the   B   M   E

3. I hear the **u** in   at the   B   M   E

4. I hear the **dr** in   at the   B   M   E

5. I hear the **s** in   at the   B   M   E

6. I hear the **u** in   at the   B   M   E

7. I hear the **g** in   at the   B   M   E

8. I hear the **r** in   at the   B   M   E

9. I hear the **u** in   at the   B   M   E

10. I hear the **h** in   at the   B   M   E

ug, um, un, us, up, ut

Name: _____

How Many Sounds Can You Hear?

Put your hand on top of the hand below. Read each of the words out loud SLOWLY. For every sound you hear, tap on a finger. How many taps were there? Circle that number.

up	2	3	4	5
chug	2	3	4	5
gun	2	3	4	5
shut	2	3	4	5
swum	2	3	4	5
plus	2	3	4	5
chum	2	3	4	5
shrug	2	3	4	5
us	2	3	4	5

ug, um, un, us, up, ut

Name: _____

Words From Earth or Mars?

Which words are real words we use on Earth? Which words are Martian words used only on Mars? Sort them.

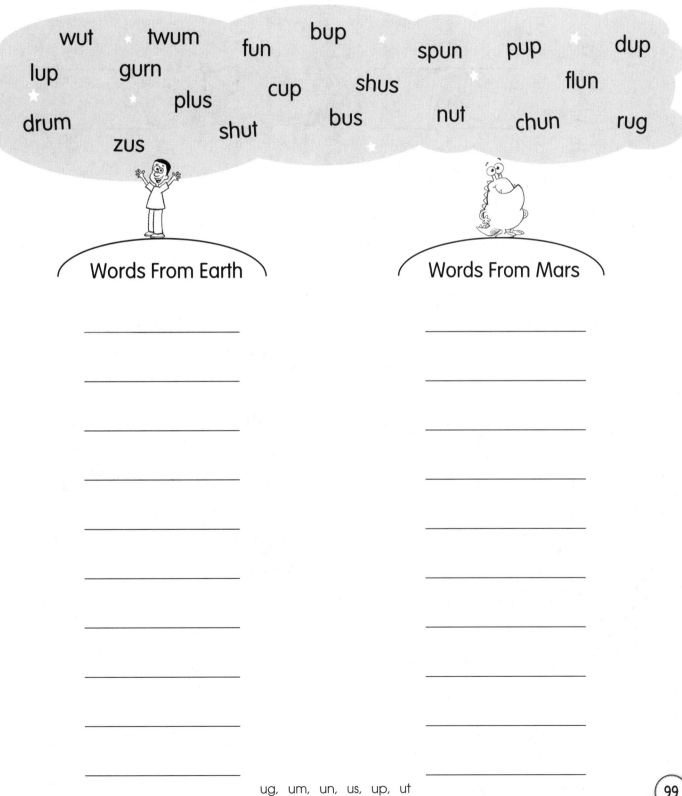

wut twum bup fun spun pup dup

lup gurn cup shus flun

plus bus nut chun rug

drum shut

zus

Words From Earth

Words From Mars

_____ _____

_____ _____

_____ _____

_____ _____

_____ _____

_____ _____

_____ _____

_____ _____

ug, um, un, us, up, ut

Name: _____

They All Sound the Same

Can you think of three rhyming words to go with each picture?

run _____
_____
_____

bus _____
_____
_____

up _____
_____
_____

gum _____
_____
_____

nut _____
_____
_____

bug _____
_____
_____

ug, um, un, us, up, ut

20 Week-by-Week Word Family Packets © 2008 by Lisa Fitzgerald McKeon, Scholastic Teaching Resources

Name: _____

What Is Missing?

Complete the sentences by using each of the letters and blends from the magnifying glass.

m   p
pl   r
g   n

1. The squirrel ate a _____ut.

2. We drank hot milk out of _____ugs.

3. You cannot have _____um at school.

4. We have had my dog since she was a little _____up.

5. Two _____us two is four.

6. At recess all of the kids love to _____un around.

ug, um, un, us, up, ut

Name: _____

Silly Sentences

Circle the silly sentences. For each silly sentence you find, color the shape with that number. What picture do you see?

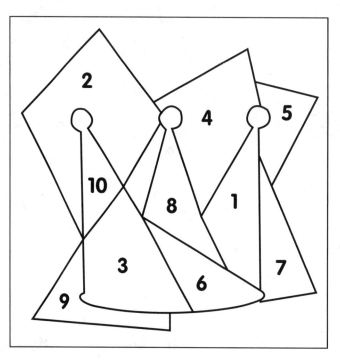

1. I had a cup of mug gum.

2. I had to run for the bus.

3. I hum in the hut and hug the bugs.

4. The hut was up on the hill.

5. He likes to eat hot dogs on buns.

6. Jug the gum and cut the rut.

7. It is up to us.

8. But the bug nut is a thug!

9. Plums are purple.

10. Drums swum in a pool of bugs.

ug, um, un, us, up, ut

Name: _____

Read, Think, Then Read Again

Read the story below. Then color the picture that goes with it.

The Pup

The pup did <u>not</u> see a big bug.

The pup did <u>not</u> see a big bus.

The pup did <u>not</u> chew gum.

The pup did have fun in the sun!

1. 2.

3. 4.

ug, um, un, us, up, ut

Name: _____

Which Spelling Is Right?

Look at each picture. Then circle the correct spelling of the word.

1.   runn
     run
     wrun

2.   cup
     kup
     cupp

3.   drm
     drum
     dum

4.   nutt
     gnut
     nut

5.   bsu
     buss
     bus

6.   plg
     plugg
     plug

ug, um, un, us, up, ut

Name: _____

vowel + consonant cluster

u + **mp** ➡ h**ump**

u + **st** ➡ d**ust**

u + **sh** ➡ br**ush**

u + **nk** ➡ sk**unk**

u + **ng** ➡ s**ung**

u + **ck** ➡ d**uck**

Checklist
✔ off each page after you complete it.

_____ Activity 1

_____ Activity 2

_____ Activity 3

_____ Activity 4

_____ Activity 5

_____ Activity 6

_____ Activity 7

_____ Activity 8

_____ Activity 9

Name: _____

Which Words Live Here?

Use the letters and blends from the attic to make words in each word family. If you can't make any more real words, you can make nonsense words.

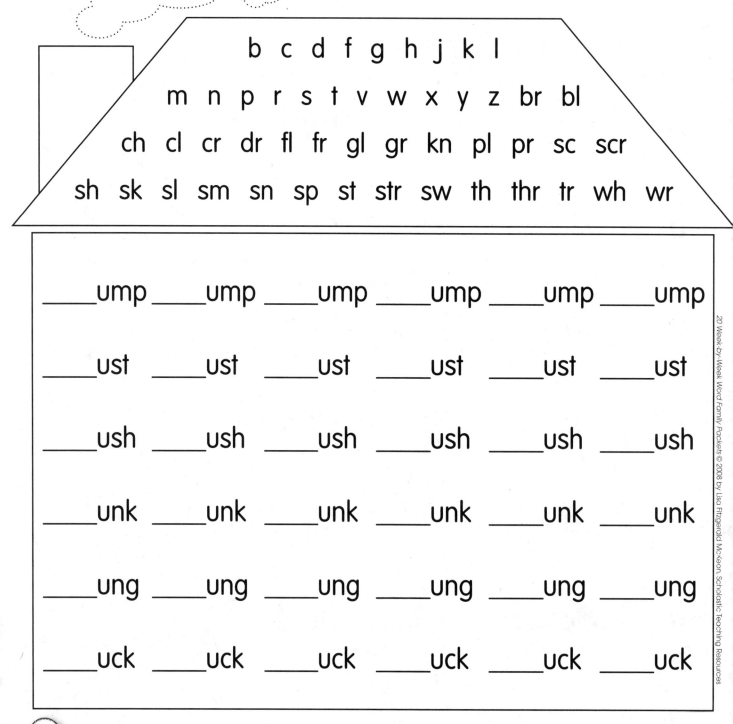

b c d f g h j k l

m n p r s t v w x y z br bl

ch cl cr dr fl fr gl gr kn pl pr sc scr

sh sk sl sm sn sp st str sw th thr tr wh wr

____ump ____ump ____ump ____ump ____ump ____ump

____ust ____ust ____ust ____ust ____ust ____ust

____ush ____ush ____ush ____ush ____ush ____ush

____unk ____unk ____unk ____unk ____unk ____unk

____ung ____ung ____ung ____ung ____ung ____ung

____uck ____uck ____uck ____uck ____uck ____uck

ump, ust, ush, unk, ung, uck

20 Week-by-Week Word Family Packets © 2008 by Lisa Fitzgerald McKeon, Scholastic Teaching Resources

Name: _____

Where Do You Hear It?

Do you hear the sound at the <u>B</u>EGINNING, <u>M</u>IDDLE, or <u>E</u>ND?
Circle the right answer.

1. I hear the **p** in   at the B   M   E

2. I hear the **s** in   at the B   M   E

3. I hear the **u** in   at the B   M   E

4. I hear the **g** in   at the B   M   E

5. I hear the **u** in   at the B   M   E

6. I hear the **u** in   at the B   M   E

7. I hear the **k** in   at the B   M   E

8. I hear the **u** in   at the B   M   E

9. I hear the **b** in   at the B   M   E

10. I hear the **d** in   at the B   M   E

20 Week-by-Week Word Family Packets © 2008 by Lisa Fitzgerald McKeon, Scholastic Teaching Resources

ump, ust, ush, unk, ung, uck

Name: _____

How Many Sounds Can You Hear?

Put your hand on top of the hand below. Read each of the words out loud SLOWLY. For every sound you hear, tap on a finger. How many taps were there? Circle that number.

junk	2	3	4	5
flung	2	3	4	5
gush	2	3	4	5
rust	2	3	4	5
pump	2	3	4	5
chuck	2	3	4	5
chunk	2	3	4	5
blush	2	3	4	5
rush	2	3	4	5

ump, ust, ush, unk, ung, uck

Name: _____

Words From Earth or Mars?

Which words are real words we use on Earth? Which words are Martian words used only on Mars? Sort them.

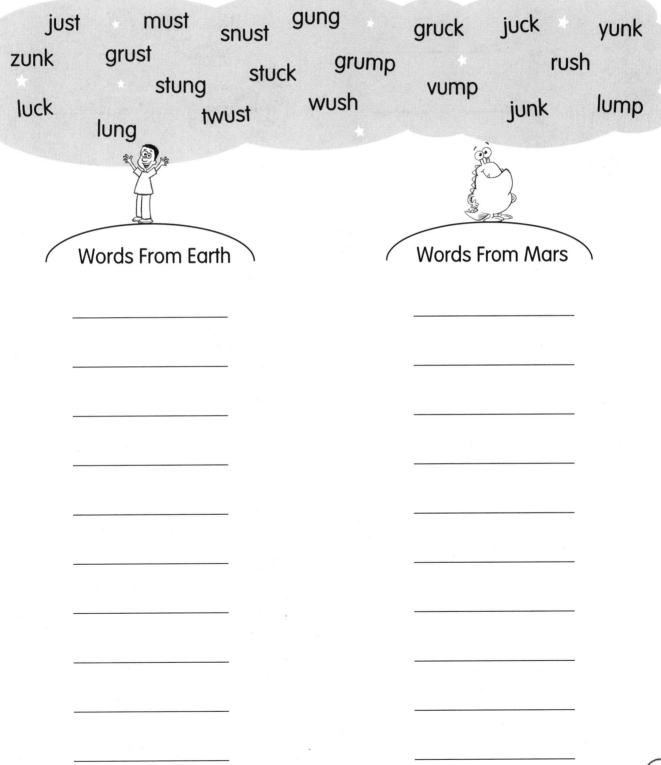

just   must   snust   gung   gruck   juck   yunk

zunk   grust   stuck   grump   rush

stung   vump

luck   wush   junk   lump

lung   twust

Words From Earth

Words From Mars

_____   _____

_____   _____

_____   _____

_____   _____

_____   _____

_____   _____

_____   _____

_____   _____

ump, ust, ush, unk, ung, uck

Name: _____

They All Sound the Same

Can you think of three rhyming words to go with each picture?

hump _____

_____

_____

skunk _____

_____

_____

dust _____

_____

_____

brush _____

_____

_____

duck _____

_____

_____

stung _____

_____

_____

ump, ust, ush, unk, ung, uck

20 Week-by-Week Word Family Packets © 2008 by Lisa Fitzgerald McKeon, Scholastic Teaching Resources

Name: _____

What Is Missing?

Complete the sentences by using each of the letters and blends from the magnifying glass.

cr   b

l   j

tr   r

1. She loves to ____ump rope.

2. I can see an X-ray of my ____ung.

3. I don't like to eat the ____ust on my sandwich.

4. For my birthday Grandpa gave me a new dump ____uck.

5. Dad said, "Hurry! We are in a ____ush!"

6. I sleep in a ____unk bed.

ump, ust, ush, unk, ung, uck

Name: _____

Silly Sentences

Circle the silly sentences. For each silly sentence you find, color the shape with that number. What picture do you see?

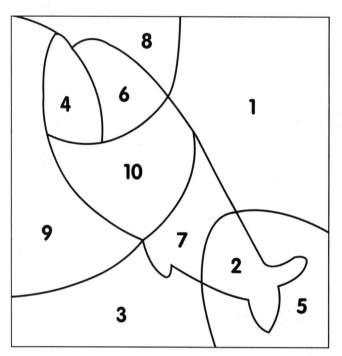

1. Do you trust me?

2. Will you brush the junk truck today?

3. There is a lot of junk in my bedroom.

4. The girl jumped on top of the flush and clung.

5. I hung up my jacket.

6. There is a lump on the skunk trunk.

7. The muck was plush and had some dust.

8. I saw a skunk and it made me jump!

9. Can you tuck me in?

10. You can trust my rush slush.

ump, ust, ush, unk, ung, uck

Name: _____

Read, Think, Then Read Again

Read the story below. Then color the picture that goes with it.

The Bunk Beds

A duck is on the top bunk.

A skunk is on the bottom bunk.

The duck is jumping.

The skunk does <u>not</u> have a toy truck.

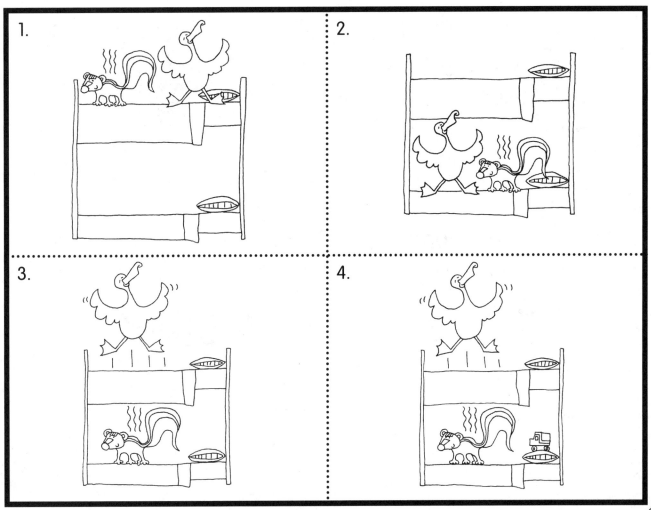

Name: _____

Which Spelling Is Right?

Look at each picture. Then circle the correct spelling of the word.

1.
jmp

gump

jump

4.
krsut

crust

krust

2.
brush

rush

prush

5.
sknk

scunk

skunk

3.
longs

lngs

lungs

6.
truck

trukc

trcku

ump, ust, ush, unk, ung, uck

Name: _____

vowel + consonant + silent e

a + ke → rake

a + le → wh**ale**

a + me → g**ame**

a + te → pl**ate**

a + pe → **ape**

a + ve → sh**ave**

Checklist

✔ off each page after you complete it.

_____ Activity 1

_____ Activity 2

_____ Activity 3

_____ Activity 4

_____ Activity 5

_____ Activity 6

_____ Activity 7

_____ Activity 8

_____ Activity 9

Name: _____

Which Words Live Here?

Use the letters and blends from the attic to make words in each word family. If you can't make any more real words, you can make nonsense words.

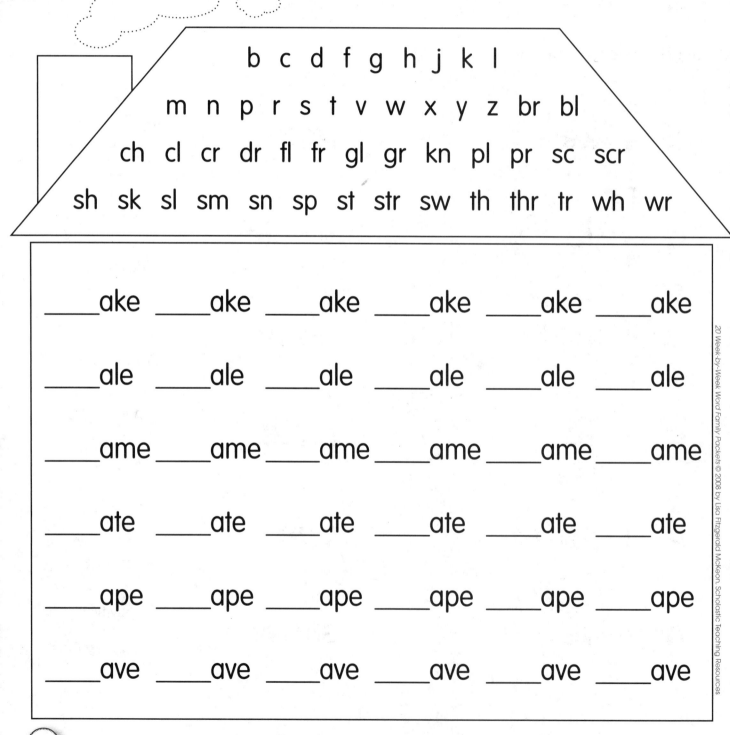

b c d f g h j k l

m n p r s t v w x y z br bl

ch cl cr dr fl fr gl gr kn pl pr sc scr

sh sk sl sm sn sp st str sw th thr tr wh wr

____ake ____ake ____ake ____ake ____ake ____ake

____ale ____ale ____ale ____ale ____ale ____ale

____ame ____ame ____ame ____ame ____ame ____ame

____ate ____ate ____ate ____ate ____ate ____ate

____ape ____ape ____ape ____ape ____ape ____ape

____ave ____ave ____ave ____ave ____ave ____ave

ake, ale, ame, ate, ape, ave

20 Week-by-Week Word Family Packets © 2008 by Lisa Fitzgerald McKeon, Scholastic Teaching Resources

Name: _____

Where Do You Hear It?

Do you hear the sound at the <u>B</u>EGINNING, <u>M</u>IDDLE, or <u>E</u>ND?
Circle the right answer.

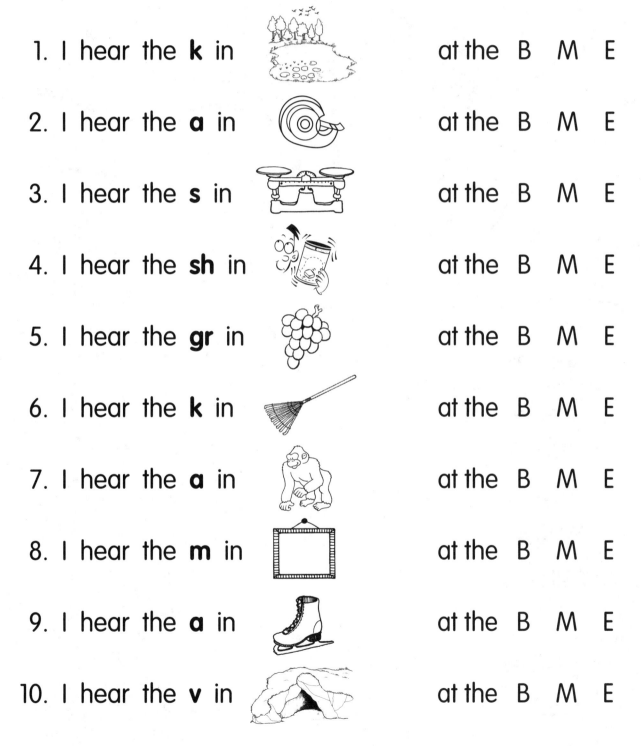

1. I hear the **k** in   at the   B   M   E

2. I hear the **a** in   at the   B   M   E

3. I hear the **s** in   at the   B   M   E

4. I hear the **sh** in   at the   B   M   E

5. I hear the **gr** in   at the   B   M   E

6. I hear the **k** in   at the   B   M   E

7. I hear the **a** in   at the   B   M   E

8. I hear the **m** in   at the   B   M   E

9. I hear the **a** in   at the   B   M   E

10. I hear the **v** in   at the   B   M   E

ake, ale, ame, ate, ape, ave

Name: _____

How Many Sounds Can You Hear?

Put your hand on top of the hand below. Read each of the words out loud SLOWLY. For every sound you hear, tap on a finger. How many taps were there? Circle that number.

	2	3	4	5
shape	2	3	4	5
blame	2	3	4	5
fake	2	3	4	5
crate	2	3	4	5
whale	2	3	4	5
ape	2	3	4	5
state	2	3	4	5
scrape	2	3	4	5
came	2	3	4	5

ake, ale, ame, ate, ape, ave

20 Week-by-Week Word Family Packets © 2008 by Lisa Fitzgerald McKeon, Scholastic Teaching Resources

Name: _____

Words From Earth or Mars?

Which words are real words we use on Earth? Which words are Martian words used only on Mars? Sort them.

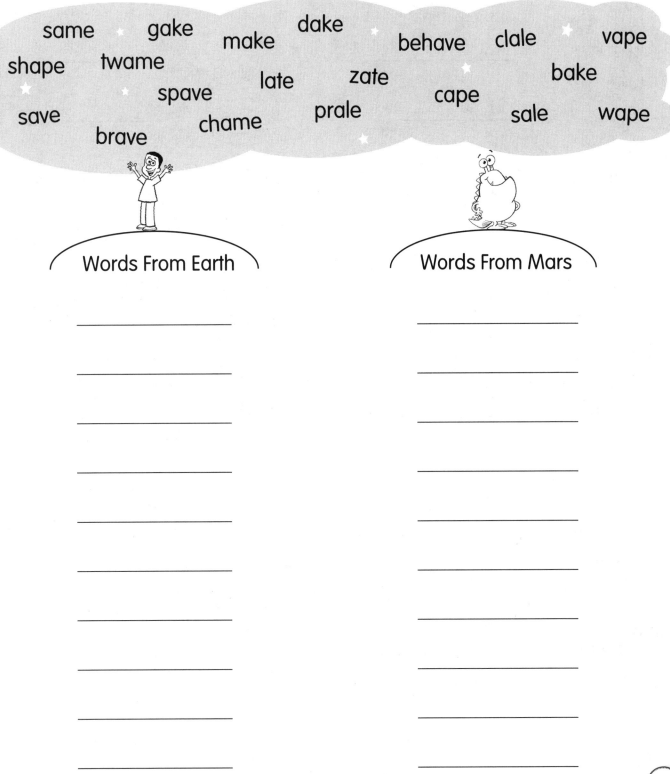

same   gake   make   dake   behave   clale   vape

shape   twame   zate   bake

late   cape

spave   save   prale   sale   wape

chame   brave

Words From Earth

Words From Mars

_____   _____

_____   _____

_____   _____

_____   _____

_____   _____

_____   _____

_____   _____

_____   _____

_____   _____

ake, ale, ame, ate, ape, ave

Activity
5
Rhyming

Name: _____

They All Sound the Same

Can you think of three rhyming words to go with each picture?

wave _____

snake _____

name _____

plate _____

grape _____

whale _____

ake, ale, ame, ate, ape, ave

20 Week-by-Week Word Family Packets © 2008 by Lisa Fitzgerald McKeon, Scholastic Teaching Resources

Name: _____

What Is Missing?

Complete the sentences by using each of the letters and blends from the magnifying glass.

g   scr

s   sh

c   wh

1. I went deep-sea fishing and we saw a ____ale!

2. My best friend has the ____ame name as me.

3. Oh no! I left the ____ate open and the dog got out!

4. My Dad has to ____ave every morning.

5. Do you like pan____akes?

6. I fell down and got a ____ape on my hand.

ake, ale, ame, ate, ape, ave

Name: _____

Silly Sentences

Circle the silly sentences. For each silly sentence you find, color the shape with that number. What picture do you see?

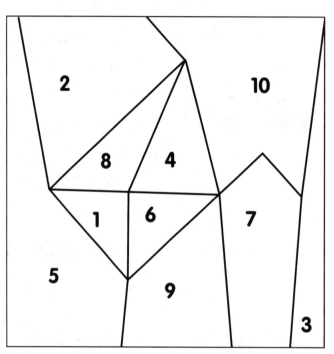

1. I put the scale on a plate and ate it.

2. Jake jumped in the big wave.

3. The ape likes grapes.

4. I gave the cupcake a grape bath.

5. I need to make my bed.

6. The sale is stale and has a scrape.

7. The snake is in the crate.

8. My brave name is a shake.

9. Can you take the rake inside?

10. I saved the cake cave for you.

ake, ale, ame, ate, ape, ave

20 Week-by-Week Word Family Packets © 2008 by Lisa Fitzgerald McKeon, Scholastic Teaching Resources

Name: _____

Read, Think, Then Read Again

Read the story below. Then color the picture that goes with it.

Jake Is Not Brave

Jake does <u>not</u> ride whales.

Jake does <u>not</u> go in lakes.

Jake does <u>not</u> take baths.

Jake does run from snakes!

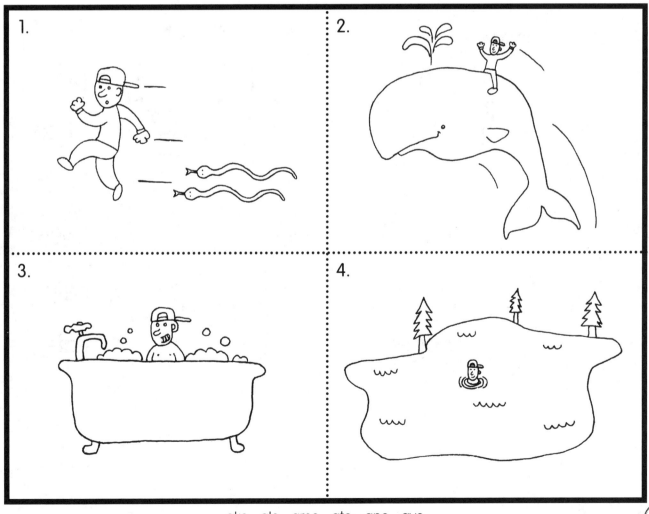

1.

2.

3.

4.

ake, ale, ame, ate, ape, ave

Name: _____

Which Spelling Is Right?

Look at each picture. Then circle the correct spelling of the word.

1. snak

    snaek

    snake

4. wahle

    whale

    whael

2. frame

    rame

    farme

5. plaet

    plat

    plate

3. papr

    paeper

    paper

6. kave

    cave

    cafe

ake, ale, ame, ate, ape, ave

Name: _____

You will learn these word families:
ay, ain, ail, ank, ang, eigh

All of these families say "A"!

ay ➡ hay

ai + n ➡ rain

ai + l ➡ nail

a + nk ➡ bank

a + ng ➡ fangs

eigh ➡ eight

Checklist

✔ off each page after you complete it.

_____ Activity 1

_____ Activity 2

_____ Activity 3

_____ Activity 4

_____ Activity 5

_____ Activity 6

_____ Activity 7

_____ Activity 8

_____ Activity 9

Name: _____

Which Words Live Here?

Use the letters and blends from the attic to make words in each word family. If you can't make any more real words, you can make nonsense words.

b c d f g h j k l

m n p r s t v w x y z br bl

ch cl cr dr fl fr gl gr kn pl pr sc scr

sh sk sl sm sn sp st str sw th thr tr wh wr

____ay   ____ay   ____ay   ____ay   ____ay   ____ay

____ain   ____ain   ____ain   ____ain   ____ain   ____ain

____ail   ____ail   ____ail   ____ail   ____ail   ____ail

____ank   ____ank   ____ank   ____ank   ____ank   ____ank

____ang   ____ang   ____ang   ____ang   ____ang   ____ang

____eigh   ____eigh   ____eigh   ____eigh   ____eigh   ____eigh

ay, ain, ail, ank, ang, eigh

20 Week-by-Week Word Family Packets © 2008 by Lisa Fitzgerald McKeon, Scholastic Teaching Resources

Name: _____

Where Do You Hear It?

Do you hear the sound at the <u>B</u>EGINNING, <u>M</u>IDDLE, or <u>E</u>ND?
Circle the right answer.

1. I hear the **t** in   at the   B   M   E

2. I hear the **a** in   at the   B   M   E

3. I hear the **a** in   at the   B   M   E

4. I hear the **l** in   at the   B   M   E

5. I hear the **p** in   at the   B   M   E

6. I hear the **a** in   at the   B   M   E

7. I hear the **br** in   at the   B   M   E

8. I hear the **s** in   at the   B   M   E

9. I hear the **k** in   at the   B   M   E

10. I hear the **sn** in   at the   B   M   E

ay, ain, ail, ank, ang, eigh

Name: _____

How Many Sounds Can You Hear?

Put your hand on top of the hand below. Read each of the words out loud SLOWLY. For every sound you hear, tap on a finger. How many taps were there? Circle that number.

	2	3	4	5
spray	2	3	4	5
chain	2	3	4	5
thank	2	3	4	5
sang	2	3	4	5
hay	2	3	4	5
gang	2	3	4	5
bank	2	3	4	5
eight	2	3	4	5
weigh	2	3	4	5

ay, ain, ail, ank, ang, eigh

20 Week-by-Week Word Family Packets © 2008 by Lisa Fitzgerald McKeon, Scholastic Teaching Resources

Name: _____

Words From Earth or Mars?

Which words are real words we use on Earth? Which words are Martian words used only on Mars? Sort them.

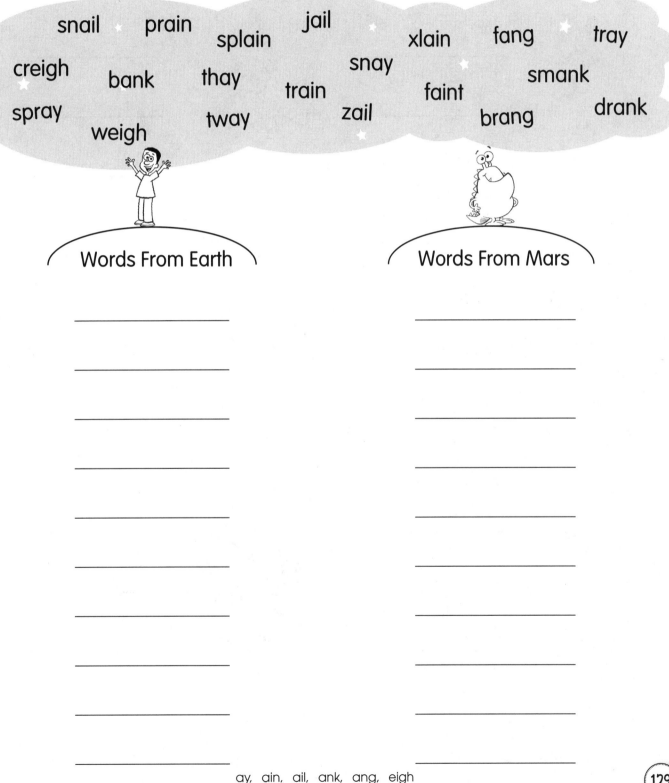

snail   prain   splain   jail   xlain   fang   tray

creigh   bank   thay   snay   smank

train   faint   drank

spray   tway   zail   brang

weigh

Words From Earth   Words From Mars

_____   _____

_____   _____

_____   _____

_____   _____

_____   _____

_____   _____

_____   _____

_____   _____

Name: _____

They All Sound the Same

Can you think of three rhyming words to go with each picture?

hay _____

fang _____

rain _____

snail _____

bank _____

sleigh _____

ay, ain, ail, ank, ang, eigh

Name: _____

What Is Missing?

Complete the sentences by using each of the letters and blends from the magnifying glass.

h   m

st   w

s   r

1. Put the letter in the ____ailbox.

2. The skunk ____ank up the house.

3. We didn't play baseball because of the ____ain.

4. Bats sleep ____anging upside down.

5. I ____eigh a lot more than my baby sister.

6. When I am mad I ____ay, "Go away!"

ay, ain, ail, ank, ang, eigh

Name: _____

Silly Sentences

Circle the silly sentences. For each silly sentence you find, color the shape with that number. What picture do you see?

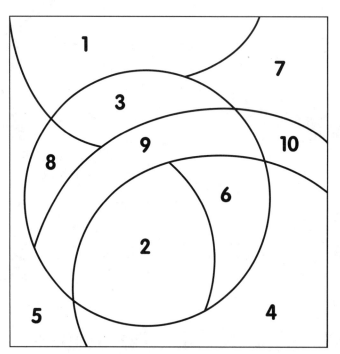

1. I saw a snail when it rained.

2. The pail is a blank clang.

3. "Twang is my rank," I say.

4. The paint spilled and made a stain.

5. The bell rang and the children sang.

6. The jail can play in his drain brain.

7. Is the crayfish gray?

8. He is a tray and a very rank tank too!

9. The grain can pay.

10. Can you go and get the mail?

ay, ain, ail, ank, ang, eigh

20 Week-by-Week Word Family Packets © 2008 by Lisa Fitzgerald McKeon, Scholastic Teaching Resources

Name: _____

Read, Think, Then Read Again

Read the story below. Then color the activity that Gail does <u>last</u>.

Gail's Day

First, Gail mailed a letter.

Then, Gail painted her house gray.

Next, Gail sang a song by her bank.

After that, Gail played with her neighbor, Hank

ay, ain, ail, ank, ang, eigh

Name: _____

Which Spelling Is Right?

Look at each picture. Then circle the correct spelling of the word.

1. trae

   tray

   traey

4. pant

   pain

   paint

2. maile

   male

   mail

5. sang

   sng

   sange

3. seigh

   slae

   sleigh

6. drnak

   darnk

   drank

ay, ain, ail, ank, ang, eigh

Name: _____

vowel + consonant + silent *e*

o + **pe** ➡ **r**ope

o + **ke** ➡ sm**oke**

o + **ve** ➡ st**ove**

o + **ne** ➡ b**one**

o + **se** ➡ r**ose**

o + **le** ➡ h**ole**

Checklist
✔ off each page after you complete it.

____ Activity 1

____ Activity 2

____ Activity 3

____ Activity 4

____ Activity 5

____ Activity 6

____ Activity 7

____ Activity 8

____ Activity 9

Name: _____

Which Words Live Here?

Use the letters and blends from the attic to make words in each word family. If you can't make any more real words, you can make nonsense words.

b c d f g h j k l

m n p r s t v w x y z br bl

ch cl cr dr fl fr gl gr kn pl pr sc scr

sh sk sl sm sn sp st str sw th thr tr wh wr

____ope ____ope ____ope ____ope ____ope ____ope

____oke ____oke ____oke ____oke ____oke ____oke

____ove ____ove ____ove ____ove ____ove ____ove

____one ____one ____one ____one ____one ____one

____ose ____ose ____ose ____ose ____ose ____ose

____ole ____ole ____ole ____ole ____ole ____ole

ope, oke, ove, one, ose, ole

Name: _____

Where Do You Hear It?

Do you hear the sound at the <u>B</u>EGINNING, <u>M</u>IDDLE, or <u>E</u>ND?
Circle the right answer.

1. I hear the **p** in   at the   B   M   E

2. I hear the **s** in   at the   B   M   E

3. I hear the **n** in   at the   B   M   E

4. I hear the **o** in   at the   B   M   E

5. I hear the **c** in   at the   B   M   E

6. I hear the **v** in   at the   B   M   E

7. I hear the **o** in   at the   B   M   E

8. I hear the **n** in   at the   B   M   E

9. I hear the **sm** in   at the   B   M   E

10. I hear the **s** in   at the   B   M   E

ope, oke, ove, one, ose, ole

Name: _____

How Many Sounds Can You Hear?

Put your hand on top of the hand below. Read each of the words out loud SLOWLY. For every sound you hear, tap on a finger. How many taps were there? Circle that number.

chose	2	3	4	5
poke	2	3	4	5
open	2	3	4	5
alone	2	3	4	5
whole	2	3	4	5
stroke	2	3	4	5
over	2	3	4	5
drove	2	3	4	5
slope	2	3	4	5

ope, oke, ove, one, ose, ole

20 Week-by-Week Word Family Packets © 2008 by Lisa Fitzgerald McKeon, Scholastic Teaching Resources

Name: _____

Words From Earth or Mars?

Which words are real words we use on Earth? Which words are Martian words used only on Mars? Sort them.

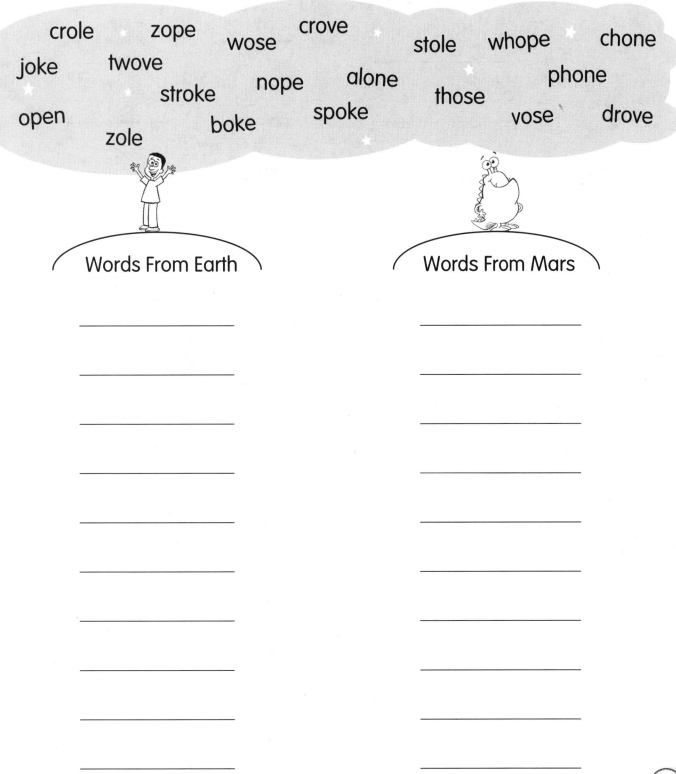

crole   zope   crove
           wose   stole   whope   chone
joke   twove
                nope   alone   phone
         stroke   those
open   boke   spoke   vose   drove
    zole

Words From Earth

Words From Mars

_____   _____

_____   _____

_____   _____

_____   _____

_____   _____

_____   _____

_____   _____

_____   _____

ope, oke, ove, one, ose, ole

Name: _____

They All Sound the Same

Can you think of three rhyming words to go with each picture?

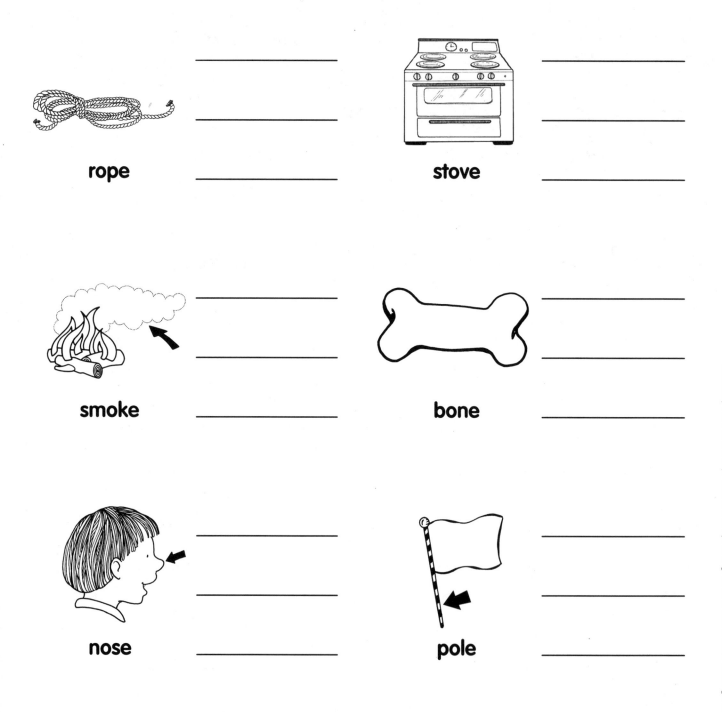

rope

stove

smoke

bone

nose

pole

ope, oke, ove, one, ose, ole

Name: _____

What Is Missing?

Complete the sentences by using each of the letters and blends from the magnifying glass.

j   b

st   m

h   ch

1. I ____ose to buy a hot dog for lunch.

2. My mom tells funny ____okes.

3. She can make pizza on her play ____ove.

4. I saw a ____ole dig a hole at the park.

5. I ____ope I get a good report card.

6. My pet dog loves to chew on his ____one.

ope, oke, ove, one, ose, ole

Name: _____

Silly Sentences

Circle the silly sentences. For each silly sentence you find, color the shape with that number. What picture do you see?

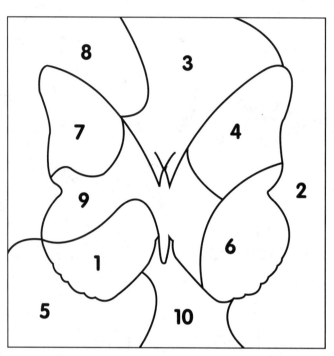

1. The choke is on the bone phone.

2. He poked him in the nose.

3. The mole ran under the rosebush.

4. I can't joke because the rope has a grove!

5. The dog hopes for some bones.

6. The stone is stole and cope.

7. The cone told a hose joke.

8. He poked her and she woke up.

9. The smoke spoke in the stove.

10. Can I have some of those?

ope, oke, ove, one, ose, ole

20 Week-by-Week Word Family Packets © 2008 by Lisa Fitzgerald McKeon, Scholastic Teaching Resources

Activity
8
Deducing

Name: _____

Read, Think, Then Read Again

Read the story below. Then color the activity that Rose does <u>last</u>.

Rose's Day

First, Rose gives her dog a bone.

Then, Rose eats a whole pizza.

Next, Rose answers the phone.

After that, Rose hears a funny joke.

ope, oke, ove, one, ose, ole

143

Name: _____

Which Spelling Is Right?

Look at each picture. Then circle the correct spelling of the word.

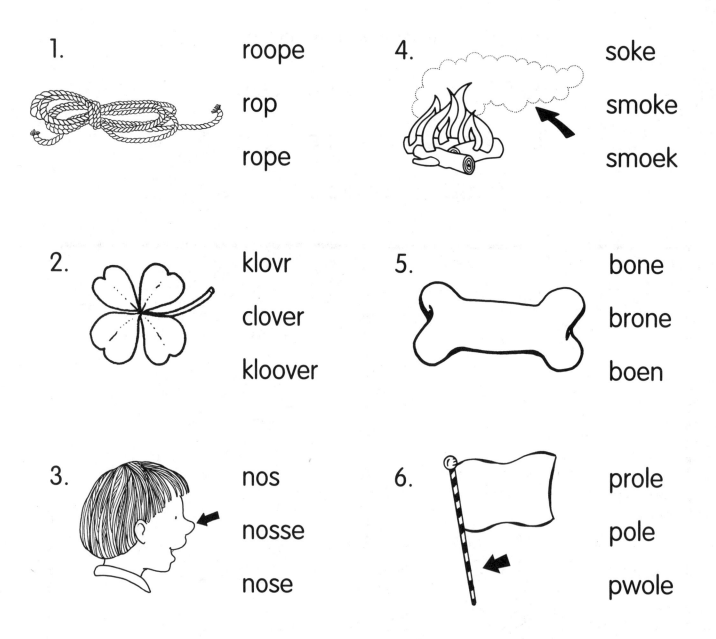

1. roope

    rop

    rope

4. soke

    smoke

    smoek

2. klovr

    clover

    kloover

5. bone

    brone

    boen

3. nos

    nosse

    nose

6. prole

    pole

    pwole

ope, oke, ove, one, ose, ole

Name: _____

All of these families say "O"!

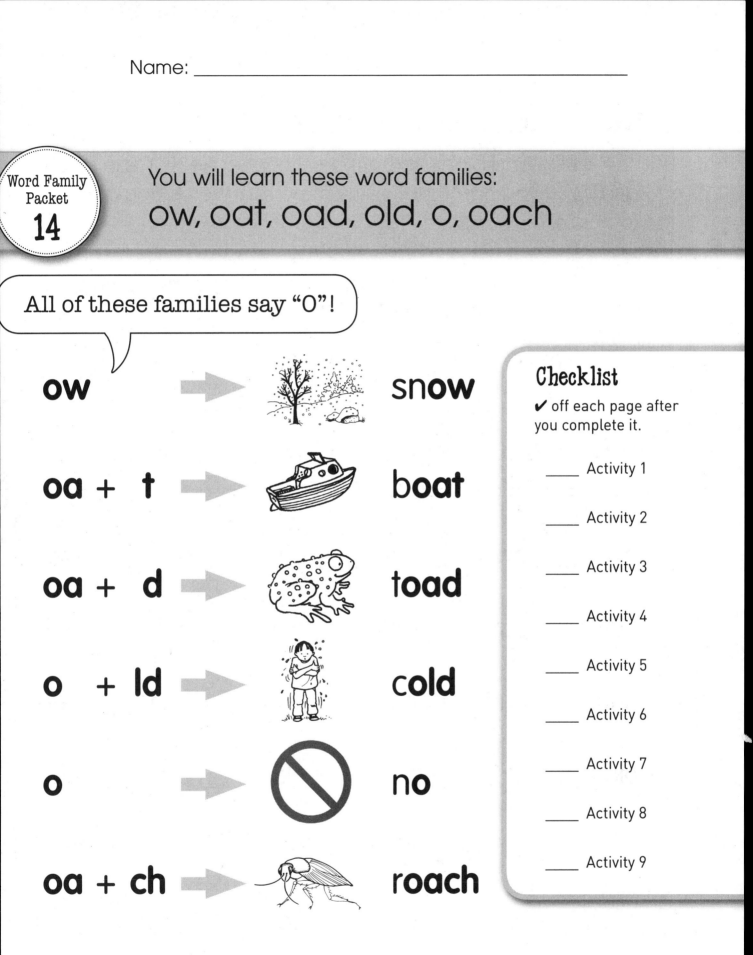

ow ➡		sn**ow**
oa + t ➡		b**oat**
oa + d ➡		t**oad**
o + ld ➡		c**old**
o ➡		n**o**
oa + ch ➡		r**oach**

Checklist

✔ off each page after you complete it.

_____ Activity 1

_____ Activity 2

_____ Activity 3

_____ Activity 4

_____ Activity 5

_____ Activity 6

_____ Activity 7

_____ Activity 8

_____ Activity 9

Name: _____

Activity
1
Blending

Which Words Live Here?

Use the letters and blends from the attic to make words in each word family. If you can't make any more real words, you can make nonsense words.

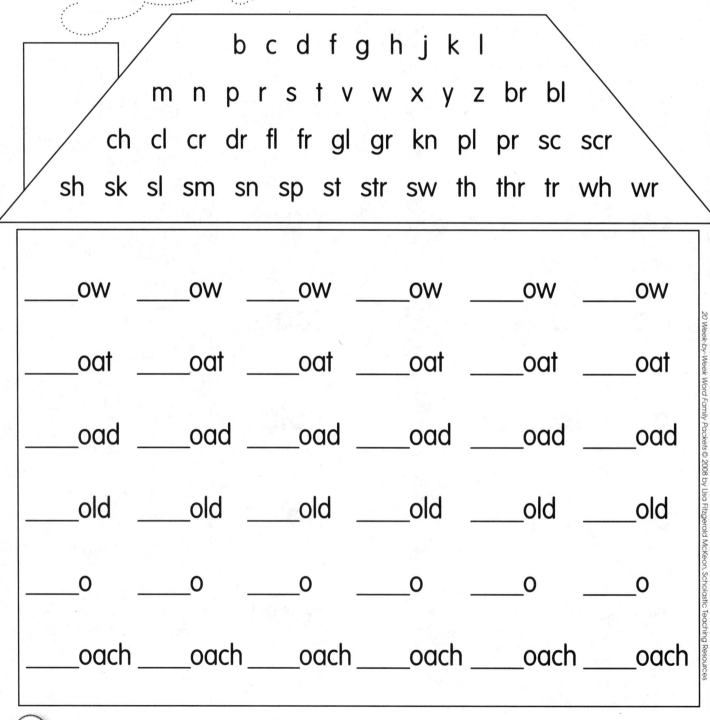

b c d f g h j k l

m n p r s t v w x y z br bl

ch cl cr dr fl fr gl gr kn pl pr sc scr

sh sk sl sm sn sp st str sw th thr tr wh wr

___ow ___ow ___ow ___ow ___ow ___ow

___oat ___oat ___oat ___oat ___oat ___oat

___oad ___oad ___oad ___oad ___oad ___oad

___old ___old ___old ___old ___old ___old

___o ___o ___o ___o ___o ___o

___oach ___oach ___oach ___oach ___oach ___oach

ow, oat, oad, old, o, oach

20 Week-by-Week Word Family Packets © 2008 by Lisa Fitzgerald McKeon, Scholastic Teaching Resources

Name: _____

Where Do You Hear It?

Do you hear the sound at the <u>B</u>EGINNING, <u>M</u>IDDLE, or <u>E</u>ND?
Circle the right answer.

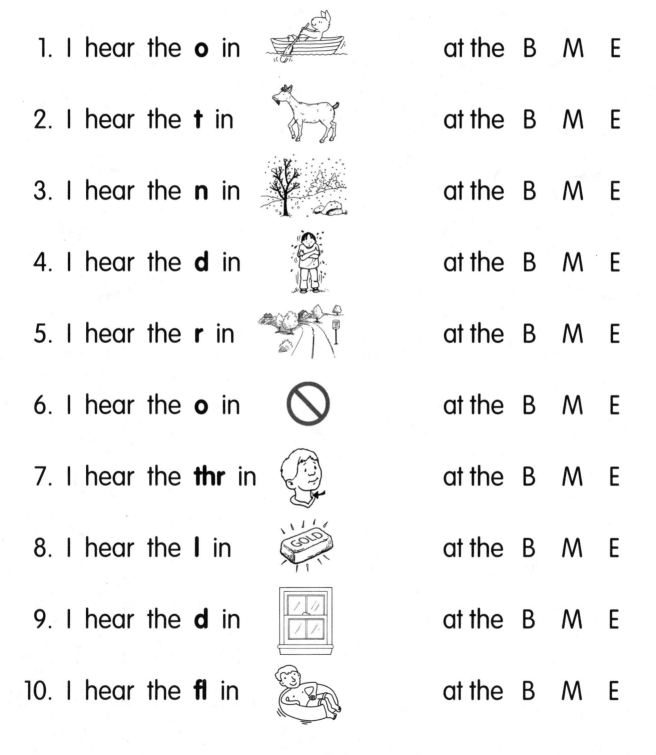

1. I hear the **o** in   at the B M E

2. I hear the **t** in   at the B M E

3. I hear the **n** in   at the B M E

4. I hear the **d** in   at the B M E

5. I hear the **r** in   at the B M E

6. I hear the **o** in   at the B M E

7. I hear the **thr** in   at the B M E

8. I hear the **l** in   at the B M E

9. I hear the **d** in   at the B M E

10. I hear the **fl** in   at the B M E

ow, oat, oad, old, o, oach

Name: _____

How Many Sounds Can You Hear?

Put your hand on top of the hand below. Read each of the words out loud SLOWLY. For every sound you hear, tap on a finger. How many taps were there? Circle that number.

coach	2	3	4	5
old	2	3	4	5
hero	2	3	4	5
know	2	3	4	5
no	2	3	4	5
throat	2	3	4	5
roach	2	3	4	5
older	2	3	4	5
window	2	3	4	5

ow, oat, oad, old, o, oach

20 Week-by-Week Word Family Packets © 2008 by Lisa Fitzgerald McKeon, Scholastic Teaching Resources

Name: _____

Words From Earth or Mars?

Which words are real words we use on Earth? Which words are Martian words used only on Mars? Sort them.

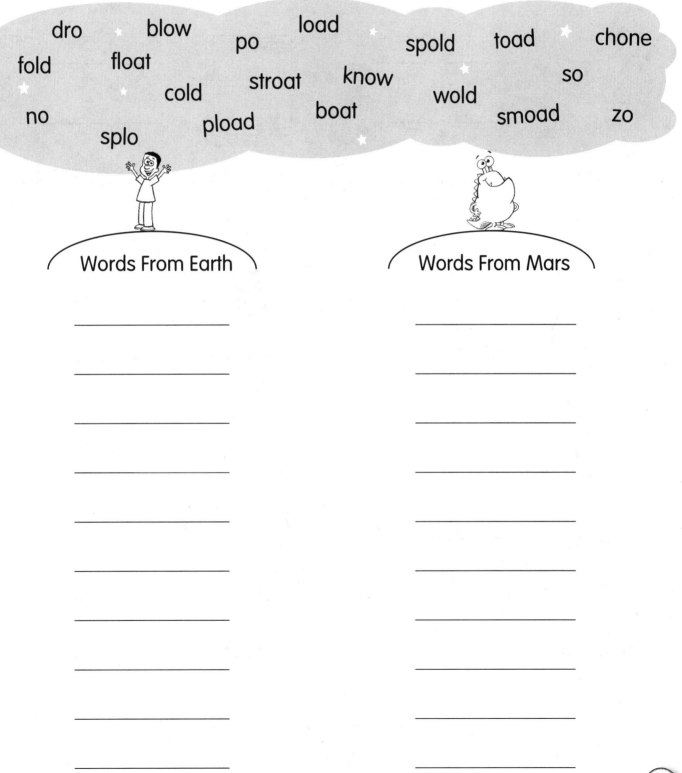

dro   blow   load   spold   toad   chone

fold   float   po   know   so

cold   stroat   wold

no   pload   boat   smoad   zo

splo

Words From Earth

Words From Mars

ow, oat, oad, old, o, oach

Name: _____

They All Sound the Same

Can you think of three rhyming words to go with each picture?

goat _____

_____

_____

window _____

_____

_____

road _____

_____

_____

cold _____

_____

_____

volcano _____

_____

coach _____

_____

ow, oat, oad, old, o, oach

20 Week-by-Week Word Family Packets © 2008 by Lisa Fitzgerald McKeon, Scholastic Teaching Resources

Name: _____

What Is Missing?

Complete the sentences by using each of the letters and blends from the magnifying glass.

f   n

t   fl

c   r

1. Please ____old your paper in half.

2. My dad is my soccer ____oach.

3. The ____oad hopped across the road.

4. The teacher has our desks in ____ows.

5. ____o! I won't go!

6. Do you know how to ____oat on your back?

20 Week-by-Week Word Family Packets © 2008 by Lisa Fitzgerald McKeon, Scholastic Teaching Resources

ow, oat, oad, old, o, oach

Name: _____

Silly Sentences

Circle the silly sentences. For each silly sentence you find, color the shape with that number. What picture do you see?

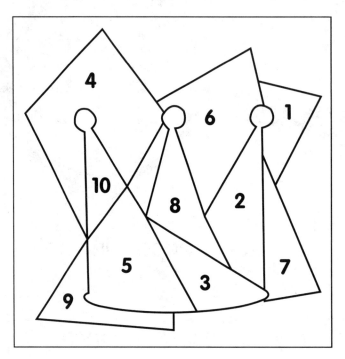

1. Go play in the snow.

2. Ago there was a row crow.

3. Your toad elbow has a glow.

4. The goat was so old.

5. I sold the cold mold.

6. It is wise to hold on to gold.

7. Kids grow slowly.

8. Fold her sold throat.

9. He was so happy to see the coach.

10. Row oats on this crow.

ow, oat, oad, old, o, oach

20 Week-by-Week Word Word Family Packets © 2008 by Lisa Fitzgerald McKeon, Scholastic Teaching Resources

Name: _____

Read, Think, Then Read Again

Read the story below. Then color the activity that the old goat does <u>last</u>.

The Old Goat's Day

First, the old goat mows the lawn.

Then, the old goat plays with a toad.

Next, the old goat rows a boat.

After that, the old goat eats oats.

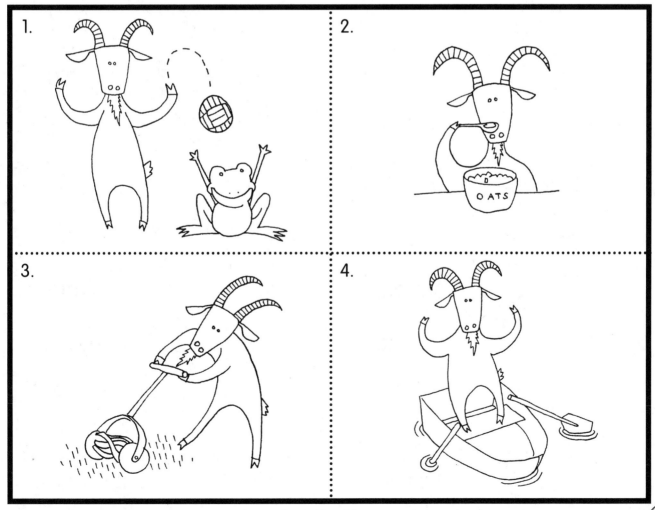

ow, oat, oad, old, o, oach

Name: _____

Which Spelling Is Right?

Look at each picture. Then circle the correct spelling of the word.

1.
sno

snowe

snow

4.
thoat

troat

throat

2.
rod

road

roade

5.
cold

kold

koald

3.
vlcano

volcano

volkano

6.
koch

koach

coach

ow, oat, oad, old, o, oach

Word Family Packet 15

You will learn these word families:
ide, ice, ine, ight, ite, y

All of these families say "I"!

i + **de** ➡ **sl**ide

i + **ce** ➡ **d**ice

i + **ne** ➡ **n**ine

i + **ght** ➡ **n**ight

i + **te** ➡ **k**ite

y ➡ **cr**y

Checklist
✔ off each page after you complete it.

____ Activity 1

____ Activity 2

____ Activity 3

____ Activity 4

____ Activity 5

____ Activity 6

____ Activity 7

____ Activity 8

____ Activity 9

Name: _____

Which Words Live Here?

Use the letters and blends from the attic to make words in each word family. If you can't make any more real words, you can make nonsense words.

b c d f g h j k l

m n p r s t v w x y z br bl

ch cl cr dr fl fr gl gr kn pl pr sc scr

sh sk sl sm sn sp st str sw th thr tr wh wr

____ide ____ide ____ide ____ide ____ide ____ide

____ice ____ice ____ice ____ice ____ice ____ice

____ine ____ine ____ine ____ine ____ine ____ine

____ight ____ight ____ight ____ight ____ight ____ight

____ite ____ite ____ite ____ite ____ite ____ite

____y ____y ____y ____y ____y ____y

ide, ice, ine, ight, ite, y

Name: _____

Where Do You Hear It?

Do you hear the sound at the <u>B</u>EGINNING, <u>M</u>IDDLE, or <u>E</u>ND?
Circle the right answer.

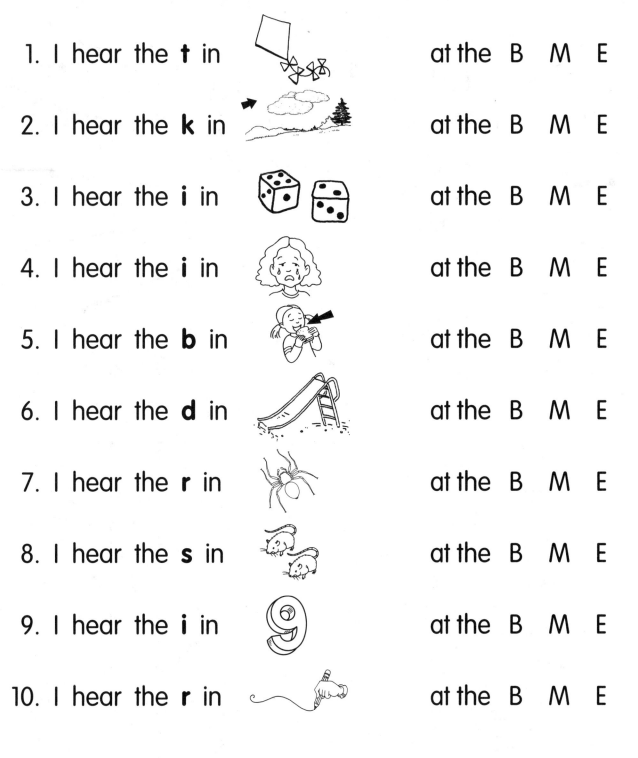

1. I hear the **t** in   at the   B   M   E

2. I hear the **k** in   at the   B   M   E

3. I hear the **i** in   at the   B   M   E

4. I hear the **i** in   at the   B   M   E

5. I hear the **b** in   at the   B   M   E

6. I hear the **d** in   at the   B   M   E

7. I hear the **r** in   at the   B   M   E

8. I hear the **s** in   at the   B   M   E

9. I hear the **i** in   at the   B   M   E

10. I hear the **r** in   at the   B   M   E

ide, ice, ine, ight, ite, y

Name: _____

How Many Sounds Can You Hear?

Put your hand on top of the hand below. Read each of the words out loud SLOWLY. For every sound you hear, tap on a finger. How many taps were there? Circle that number.

glide	2	3	4	5
ice	2	3	4	5
shine	2	3	4	5
knight	2	3	4	5
tighter	2	3	4	5
side	2	3	4	5
sky	2	3	4	5
write	2	3	4	5
my	2	3	4	5

ide, ice, ine, ight, ite, y

20 Week-by-Week Word Family Packets © 2008 by Lisa Fitzgerald McKeon, Scholastic Teaching Resources

Name: _____

Words From Earth or Mars?

Which words are real words we use on Earth? Which words are Martian words used only on Mars? Sort them.

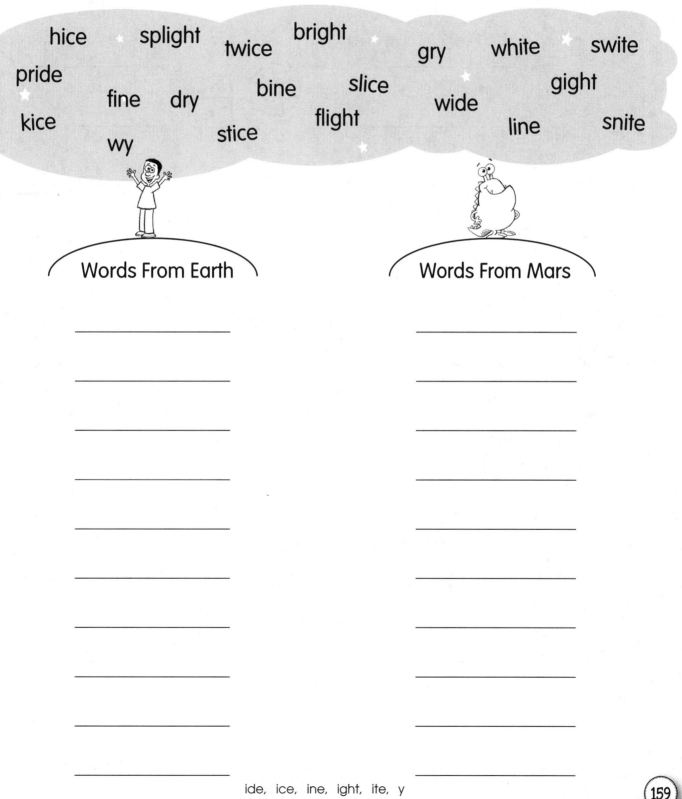

hice   splight   bright   gry   white   swite

twice

pride   bine   slice   gight

fine   dry   wide

kice   flight   line   snite

wy   stice

Words From Earth

Words From Mars

_____   _____

_____   _____

_____   _____

_____   _____

_____   _____

_____   _____

_____   _____

_____   _____

ide, ice, ine, ight, ite, y

Name: _____

They All Sound the Same

Can you think of three rhyming words to go with each picture?

hide _____

dice _____

nine _____

knight _____

cry _____

kite _____

ide, ice, ine, ight, ite, y

Name: _____

What Is Missing?

Complete the sentences by using each of the letters and blends from the magnifying glass.

r h

b fl

l n

1. "Miss Baker, she cut me in ____ine!"

2. At the park, we ran around and played

 ____ide-and-seek.

3. The ____ight light helps me to find my bed.

4. I took a big ____ite of the apple.

5. We ate chicken and ____ice.

6. I wish I knew how to ____y in the sky!

ide, ice, ine, ight, ite, y

Name: _____

Silly Sentences

Circle the silly sentences. For each silly sentence you find, color the shape with that number. What picture do you see?

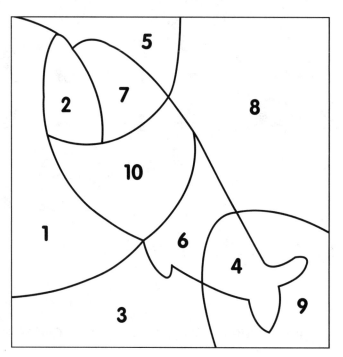

1. Those dice are mine!

2. The line has white rides on it.

3. The baby would cry at night.

4. The knight can be quite a sly sky.

5. I might get a night light.

6. The ice bright has lightning.

7. The slice has fine dice.

8. My friend is shy.

9. The red kite can fly in the sky!

10. Why does the spry bride fry on the slide?

ide, ice, ine, ight, ite, y

20 Week-by-Week Word Family Packets © 2008 by Lisa Fitzgerald McKeon, Scholastic Teaching Resources

Name: _____

Read, Think, Then Read Again

Read the story below. Then color the picture that goes with it.

The Knight and His Kite

The knight has a kite.

The kite has five spiders on it.

The kite has <u>no</u> mice on it.

The knight flies his kite at night.

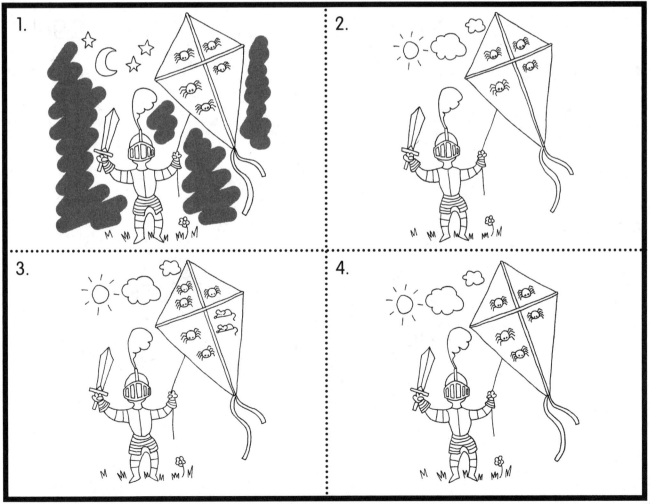

ide, ice, ine, ight, ite, y

Name: _____

Which Spelling Is Right?

Look at each picture. Then circle the correct spelling of the word.

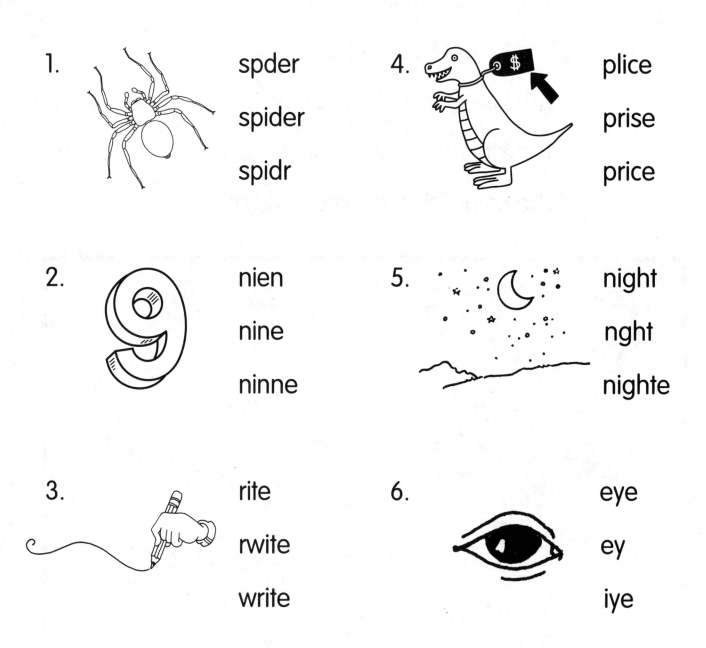

1. spder

   spider

   spidr

2. nien

   nine

   ninne

3. rite

   rwite

   write

4. plice

   prise

   price

5. night

   nght

   nighte

6. eye

   ey

   iye

ide, ice, ine, ight, ite, y

Name: _____

All of these families say "E"!

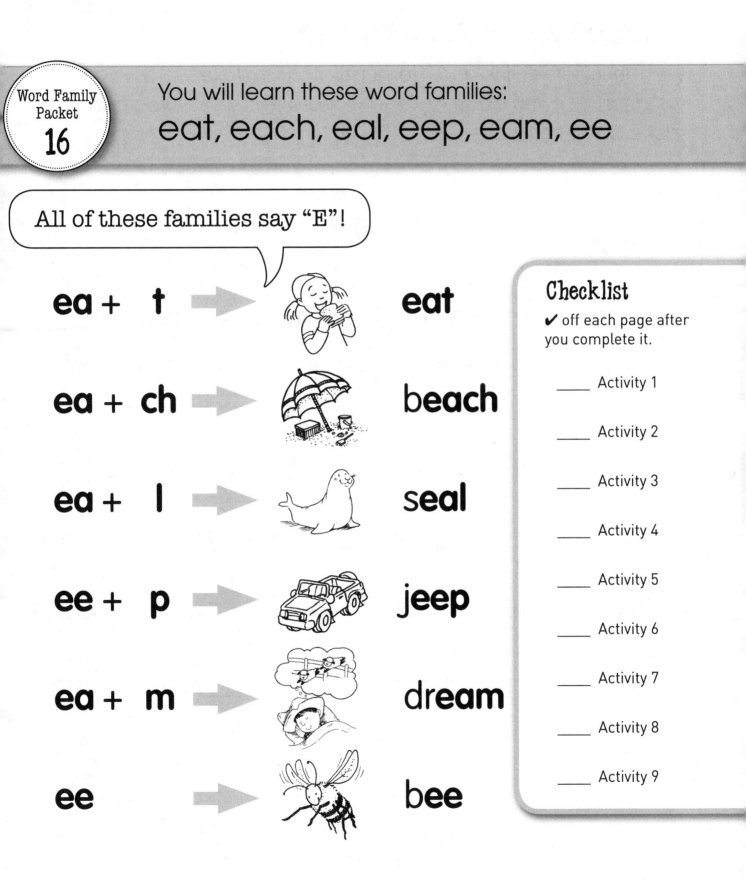

ea + t ➡ eat

ea + ch ➡ b**each**

ea + l ➡ s**eal**

ee + p ➡ j**eep**

ea + m ➡ dr**eam**

ee ➡ b**ee**

Checklist
✔ off each page after you complete it.

_____ Activity 1

_____ Activity 2

_____ Activity 3

_____ Activity 4

_____ Activity 5

_____ Activity 6

_____ Activity 7

_____ Activity 8

_____ Activity 9

Name: _____

Which Words Live Here?

Use the letters and blends from the attic to make words in each word family. If you can't make any more real words, you can make nonsense words.

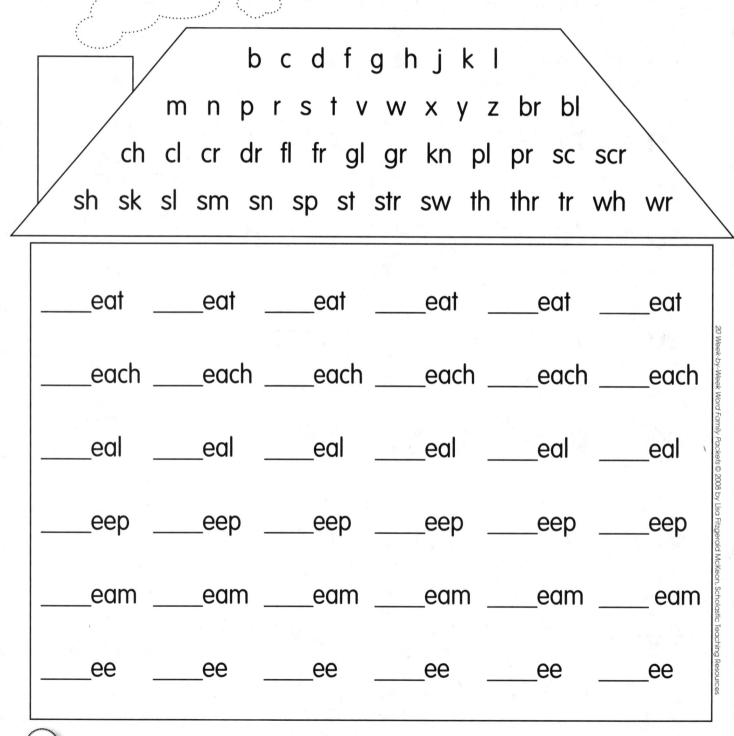

b c d f g h j k l

m n p r s t v w x y z br bl

ch cl cr dr fl fr gl gr kn pl pr sc scr

sh sk sl sm sn sp st str sw th thr tr wh wr

____eat ____eat ____eat ____eat ____eat ____eat

____each ____each ____each ____each ____each ____each

____eal ____eal ____eal ____eal ____eal ____eal

____eep ____eep ____eep ____eep ____eep ____eep

____eam ____eam ____eam ____eam ____eam ____eam

____ee ____ee ____ee ____ee ____ee ____ee

eat, each, eal, eep, eam, ee

Name: _____

Where Do You Hear It?

Do you hear the sound at the <u>B</u>EGINNING, <u>M</u>IDDLE, or <u>E</u>ND?
Circle the right answer.

1. I hear the **ch** in   at the   B   M   E

2. I hear the **e** in   at the   B   M   E

3. I hear the **l** in   at the   B   M   E

4. I hear the **e** in   at the   B   M   E

5. I hear the **b** in   at the   B   M   E

6. I hear the **scr** in   at the   B   M   E

7. I hear the **s** in   at the   B   M   E

8. I hear the **b** in   at the   B   M   E

9. I hear the **e** in   at the   B   M   E

10. I hear the **r** in   at the   B   M   E

eat, each, eal, eep, eam, ee

Name: _____

How Many Sounds Can You Hear?

Put your hand on top of the hand below. Read each of the words out loud SLOWLY. For every sound you hear, tap on a finger. How many taps were there? Circle that number.

pleat	2	3	4	5
sheep	2	3	4	5
see	2	3	4	5
teacher	2	3	4	5
seat	2	3	4	5
squeal	2	3	4	5
agree	2	3	4	5
cream	2	3	4	5
reach	2	3	4	5

eat, each, eal, eep, eam, ee

20 Week-by-Week Word Family Packets © 2008 by Lisa Fitzgerald McKeon, Scholastic Teaching Resources

Name: _____

Words From Earth or Mars?

Which words are real words we use on Earth? Which words are Martian words used only on Mars? Sort them.

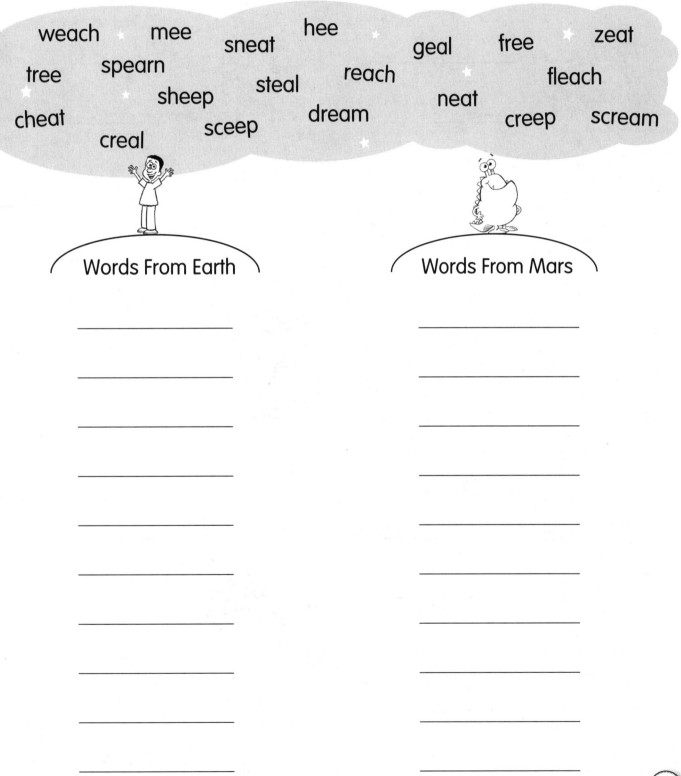

weach   mee   sneat   hee   geal   free   zeat
tree   spearn   steal   reach   fleach
cheat   sheep   dream   neat   creep   scream
creal   sceep

Words From Earth

Words From Mars

eat, each, eal, eep, eam, ee

Name: _____

They All Sound the Same

Can you think of three rhyming words to go with each picture?

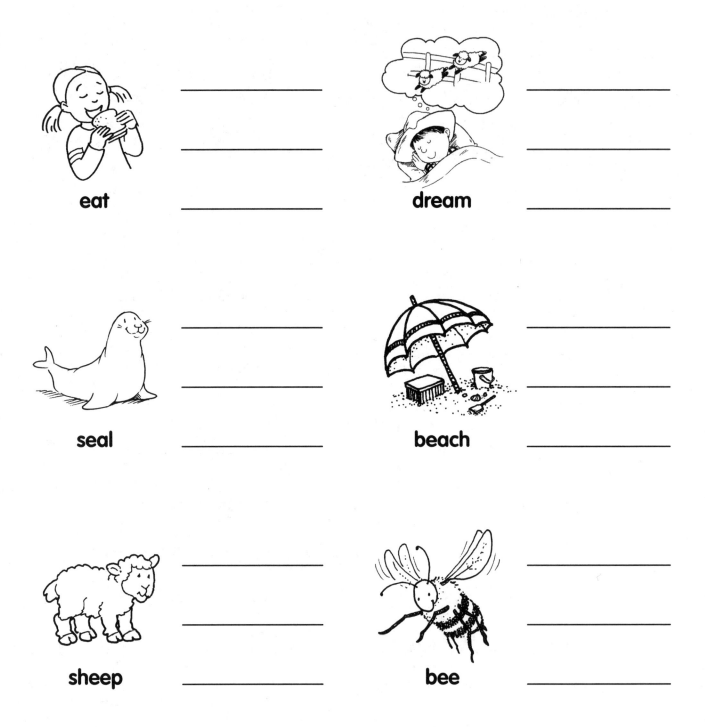

eat

_____
_____
_____

dream

_____
_____
_____

seal

_____
_____
_____

beach

_____
_____
_____

sheep

_____
_____
_____

bee

_____
_____
_____

eat, each, eal, eep, eam, ee

Name: _____

What Is Missing?

Complete the sentences by using each of the letters and blends from the magnifying glass.

dr   tr

j   thr

b   s

1. The _____eal had a ball on his nose.

2. "Trick or _____eat, smell my feet, give me something good to eat!"

3. We love to make sand castles at the _____each.

4. "One, two, _____ee! Come and get me!"

5. Mr. Jones got a brand new red _____eep.

6. I had the best _____eam last night!

eat, each, eal, eep, eam, ee

Name: _____

Silly Sentences

Circle the silly sentences. For each silly sentence you find, color the shape with that number.

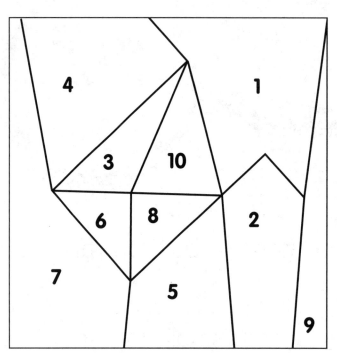

1. I like to bleach my jeep peaches before I eat them.

2. My sister is sixteen.

3. Do sheep have seal knees for peeping over fences?

4. I had a bad dream.

5. I like to keep my desk neat.

6. The seat was a treat for meat.

7. The jeep went beep.

8. My teacher eats cleats and trees.

9. Do you know how to sweep?

10. The seal wheat the beam.

eat, each, eal, eep, eam, ee

20 Week-by-Week Word Family Packets © 2008 by Lisa Fitzgerald McKeon, Scholastic Teaching Resources

Name: _____

Read, Think, Then Read Again

Read the story below. Then color the picture that goes with it.

What Lee Sees

Lee does <u>not</u> see a seal.

Lee does <u>not</u> see a sheep.

Lee does <u>not</u> eat a peach.

Lee only sleeps!

eat, each, eal, eep, eam, ee

Name: _____

Which Spelling Is Right?

Look at each picture. Then circle the correct spelling of the word.

1. steal

   seal

   sele

2. swep

   sweep

   swepe

3. sixten

   sixeteen

   sixteen

4. kneet

   nete

   neat

5. teecher

   teachr

   teacher

6. dream

   deam

   dreme

eat, each, eal, eep, eam, ee

Name: _____

All of these families say "U"!

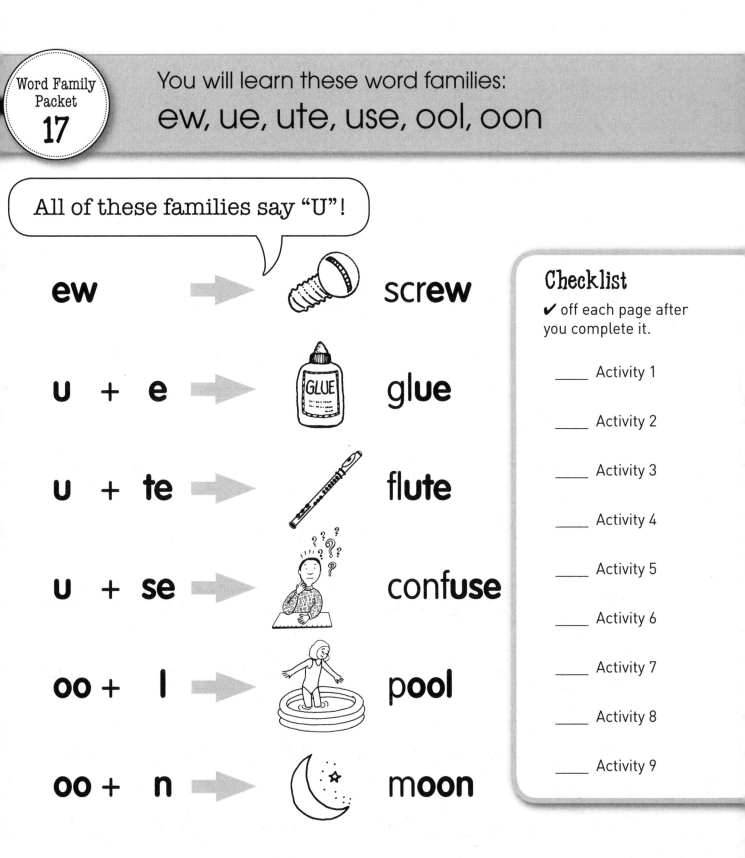

ew	➜		**screw**
u + e	➜		**glue**
u + te	➜		**flute**
u + se	➜		**confuse**
oo + l	➜		**pool**
oo + n	➜		**moon**

Checklist
✔ off each page after you complete it.

_____ Activity 1

_____ Activity 2

_____ Activity 3

_____ Activity 4

_____ Activity 5

_____ Activity 6

_____ Activity 7

_____ Activity 8

_____ Activity 9

Name: _____

Which Words Live Here?

Use the letters and blends from the attic to make words in each word family. If you can't make any more real words, you can make nonsense words.

b c d f g h j k l

m n p r s t v w x y z br bl

ch cl cr dr fl fr gl gr kn pl pr sc scr

sh sk sl sm sn sp st str sw th thr tr wh wr

_____ew _____ew _____ew _____ew _____ew _____ew

_____ue _____ue _____ue _____ue _____ue _____ue

_____ute _____ute _____ute _____ute _____ute _____ute

_____use _____use _____use _____use _____use _____use

_____ool _____ool _____ool _____ool _____ool _____ool

_____oon _____oon _____oon _____oon _____oon _____oon

ew, ue, ute, use, ool, oon

20 Week-by-Week Word Family Packets © 2008 by Lisa Fitzgerald McKeon, Scholastic Teaching Resources

Name: _____

Where Do You Hear It?

Do you hear the sound at the <u>B</u>EGINNING, <u>M</u>IDDLE, or <u>E</u>ND?
Circle the right answer.

1. I hear the **u** in   at the   B   M   E

2. I hear the **g** in   at the   B   M   E

3. I hear the **t** in   at the   B   M   E

4. I hear the **n** in   at the   B   M   E

5. I hear the **l** in   at the   B   M   E

6. I hear the **m** in   at the   B   M   E

7. I hear the **r** in   at the   B   M   E

8. I hear the **l** in   at the   B   M   E

9. I hear the **s** in   at the   B   M   E

10. I hear the **t** in   at the   B   M   E

ew, ue, ute, use, ool, oon

Name: _____

How Many Sounds Can You Hear?

Put your hand on top of the hand below. Read each of the words out loud SLOWLY. For every sound you hear, tap on a finger. How many taps were there? Circle that number.

flute	2	3	4	5
drool	2	3	4	5
use	2	3	4	5
noon	2	3	4	5
value	2	3	4	5
reuse	2	3	4	5
true	2	3	4	5
soon	2	3	4	5
threw	2	3	4	5

ew, ue, ute, use, ool, oon

Name: _____

Words From Earth or Mars?

Which words are real words we use on Earth? Which words are
Martian words used only on Mars? Sort them.

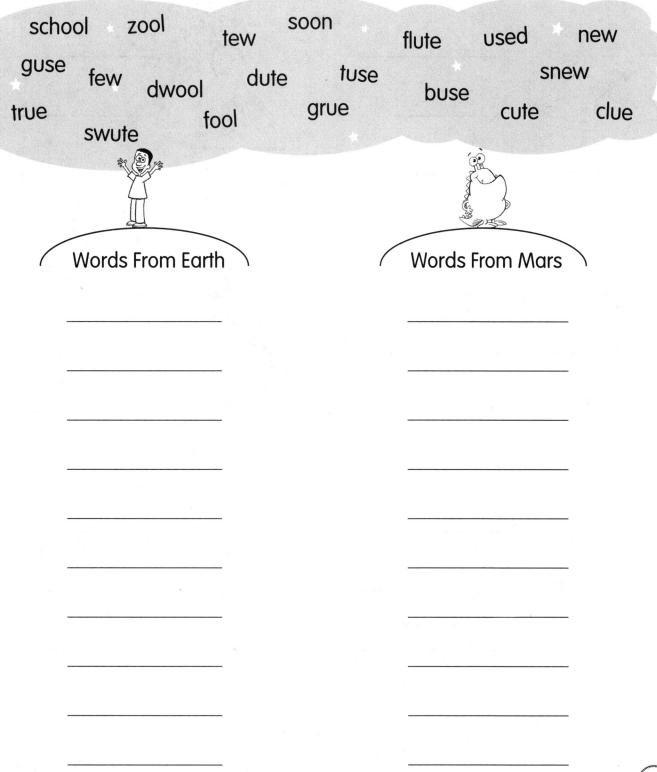

school   zool   soon   tew   flute   used   new

guse   few   dute   tuse   snew

dwool   buse

true   grue   cute   clue

swute   fool

Words From Earth

Words From Mars

_____   _____

_____   _____

_____   _____

_____   _____

_____   _____

_____   _____

_____   _____

_____   _____

_____   _____

ew, ue, ute, use, ool, oon

Name: _____

They All Sound the Same

Can you think of three rhyming words to go with each picture?

pool _____

_____

confuse _____

_____

moon _____

_____

flute _____

_____

glue _____

_____

screw _____

_____

ew, ue, ute, use, ool, oon

Name: _____

What Is Missing?

Complete the sentences by using each of the letters and blends from the magnifying glass.

m   p
d   fl
bl   n

1. I am learning how to play the ____ute.

2. Our dog likes to bark at the ____oon.

3. The ____ool is very deep.

4. He bought a ____ew blanket for his bed.

5. My favorite color in the world is ____ue.

6. She use_____ my crayons.

ew, ue, ute, use, ool, oon

Name: _____

Silly Sentences

Circle the silly sentences. For each silly sentence you find, color the shape with that number. What picture do you see?

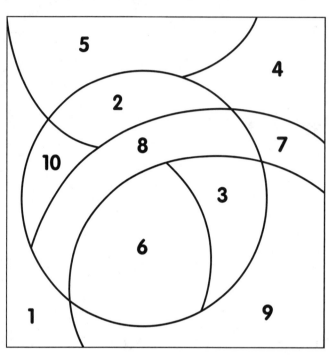

1. I am going to a new school.

2. Stew that cute flute.

3. Don't drool on pool screws.

4. Is that true?

5. Mom got a tool to fix the stool.

6. Soon the moon will flew.

7. The baby uses a new spoon.

8. The statue threw blue stew at me.

9. She drew a cute cartoon.

10. Glue and chew a few noons.

ew, ue, ute, use, ool, oon

20 Week-by-Week Word Family Packets © 2008 by Lisa Fitzgerald McKeon, Scholastic Teaching Resources

Name: _____

Read, Think, Then Read Again

Read the story below. Then color the picture that goes with it.

What Sue Likes to Do

Sue does <u>not</u> use a spoon.

Sue does <u>not</u> use tools.

Sue does <u>not</u> use a new guitar.

Sue does use a pool.

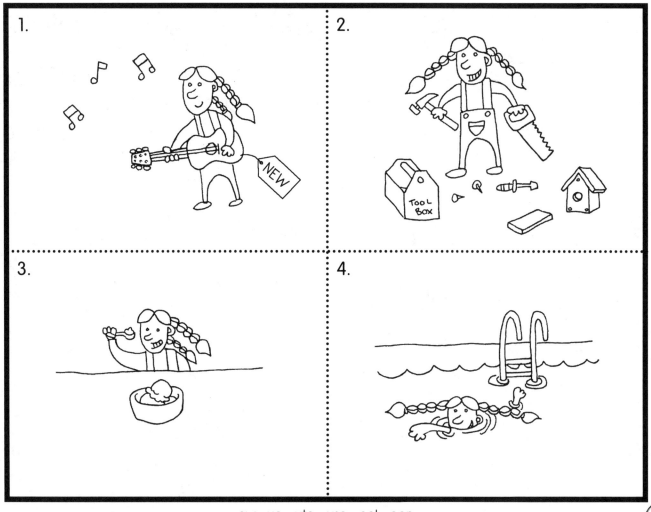

ew, ue, ute, use, ool, oon

Name: _____

Which Spelling Is Right?

Look at each picture. Then circle the correct spelling of the word.

1.
scew

scrue

screw

4.
glue

glew

gloo

2.
kute

kyute

cute

5.
konfusd

kunfused

confused

3.
shcool

school

schoole

6.
spoon

soon

spune

ew, ue, ute, use, ool, oon

Name: _____

You will learn these word families:
ar, ark, irt, ore, orn, urt

All of these families have a "bossy R"!

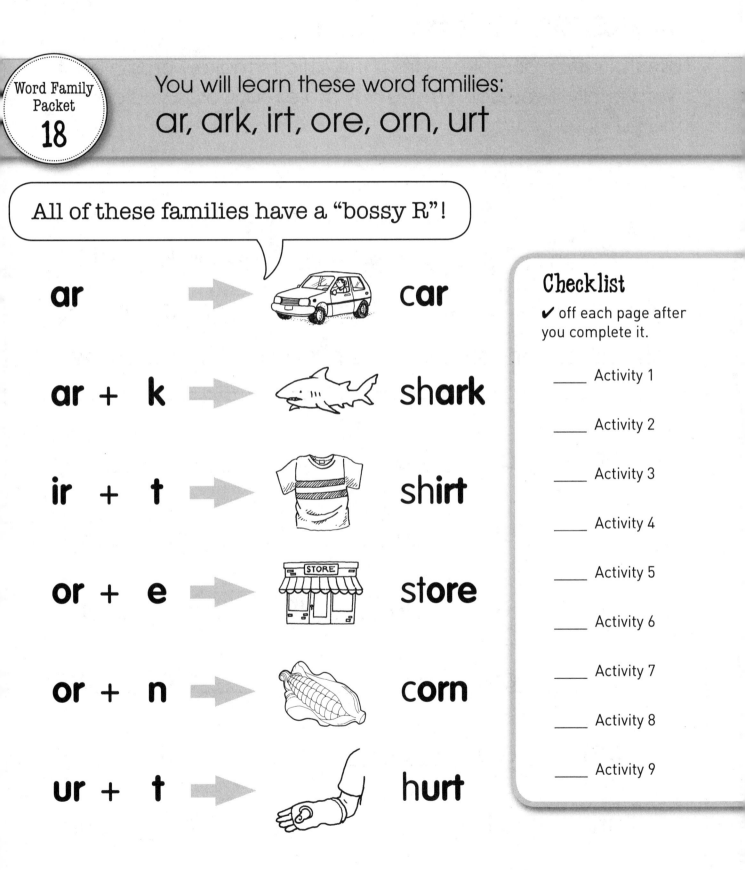

ar ➡ car

ar + k ➡ shark

ir + t ➡ shirt

or + e ➡ store

or + n ➡ corn

ur + t ➡ hurt

Checklist
✔ off each page after you complete it.

____ Activity 1

____ Activity 2

____ Activity 3

____ Activity 4

____ Activity 5

____ Activity 6

____ Activity 7

____ Activity 8

____ Activity 9

Name: _____

Which Words Live Here?

Use the letters and blends from the attic to make words in each word family. If you can't make any more real words, you can make nonsense words.

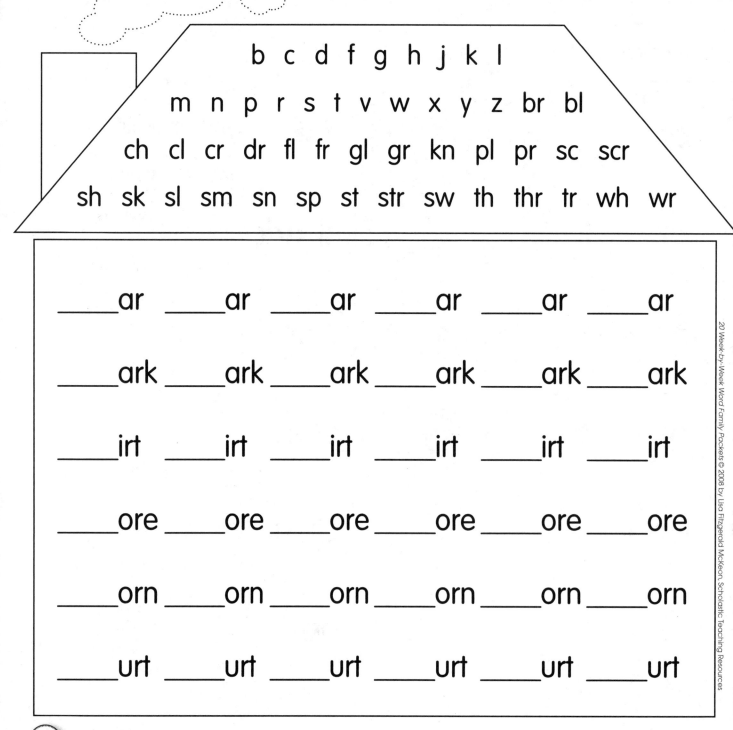

b c d f g h j k l

m n p r s t v w x y z br bl

ch cl cr dr fl fr gl gr kn pl pr sc scr

sh sk sl sm sn sp st str sw th thr tr wh wr

____ar ____ar ____ar ____ar ____ar ____ar

____ark ____ark ____ark ____ark ____ark ____ark

____irt ____irt ____irt ____irt ____irt ____irt

____ore ____ore ____ore ____ore ____ore ____ore

____orn ____orn ____orn ____orn ____orn ____orn

____urt ____urt ____urt ____urt ____urt ____urt

ar, ark, irt, ore, orn, urt

20 Week-by-Week Word Family Packets © 2008 by Lisa Fitzgerald McKeon, Scholastic Teaching Resources

Name: _____

Where Do You Hear It?

Do you hear the sound at the BEGINNING, MIDDLE, or END?
Circle the right answer.

1. I hear the **r** in [image]   at the   B   M   E

2. I hear the **c** in [image]   at the   B   M   E

3. I hear the **sh** in [image]   at the   B   M   E

4. I hear the **r** in [image]   at the   B   M   E

5. I hear the **or** in [image]   at the   B   M   E

6. I hear the **t** in [image]   at the   B   M   E

7. I hear the **r** in [image]   at the   B   M   E

8. I hear the **k** in [image]   at the   B   M   E

9. I hear the **sn** in [image]   at the   B   M   E

10. I hear the **t** in [image]   at the   B   M   E

ar, ark, irt, ore, orn, urt

Name: _____

How Many Sounds Can You Hear?

Put your hand on top of the hand below. Read each of the words out loud SLOWLY. For every sound you hear, tap on a finger. How many taps were there? Circle that number.

	2	3	4	5
star	2	3	4	5
acorn	2	3	4	5
hurt	2	3	4	5
store	2	3	4	5
spark	2	3	4	5
skirt	2	3	4	5
born	2	3	4	5
dirt	2	3	4	5
dirty	2	3	4	5

ar, ark, irt, ore, orn, urt

20 Week-by-Week Word Family Packets © 2008 by Lisa Fitzgerald McKeon, Scholastic Teaching Resources

Name: _____

Words From Earth or Mars?

Which words are real words we use on Earth? Which words are Martian words used only on Mars? Sort them.

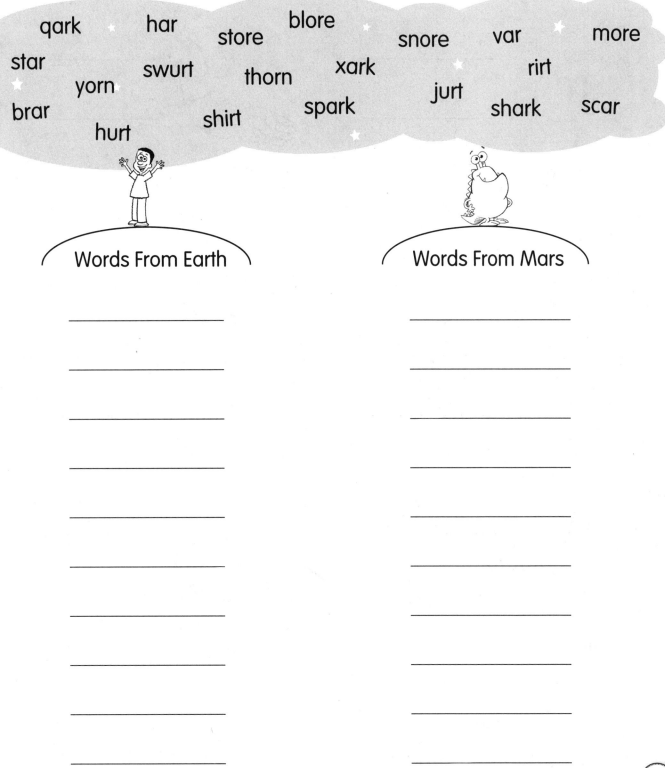

qark   har   store   blore   snore   var   more

star   swurt   thorn   xark   rirt

yorn   jurt   shark   scar

brar   shirt   spark

hurt

Words From Earth

_____

_____

_____

_____

_____

_____

_____

_____

_____

Words From Mars

_____

_____

_____

_____

_____

_____

_____

_____

_____

ar, ark, irt, ore, orn, urt

Name: _____

They All Sound the Same

Can you think of three rhyming words to go with each picture?

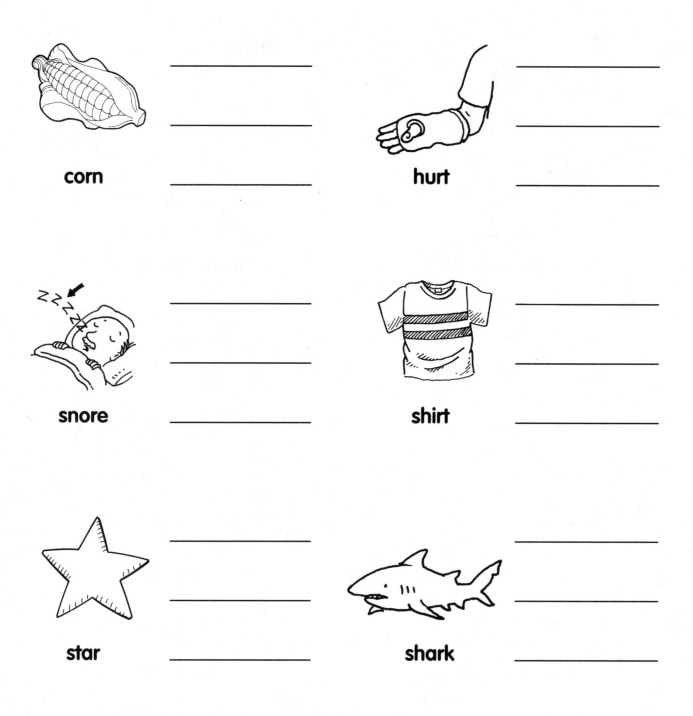

corn

_____
_____
_____

hurt

_____
_____
_____

snore

_____
_____
_____

shirt

_____
_____
_____

star

_____
_____
_____

shark

_____
_____
_____

ar, ark, irt, ore, orn, urt

20 Week-by-Week Word Family Packets © 2008 by Lisa Fitzgerald McKeon, Scholastic Teaching Resources

Name: _____

What Is Missing?

Complete the sentences by using each of the letters and blends from the magnifying glass.

m   h
st   sh
c   p

1. A bad sunburn can really ____urt!

2. I love to eat ____orn on the cob.

3. I saw a ____ar up in the sky.

4. This ____ark has the best swing set.

5. I love the ____irt you are wearing!

6. May I please have ____ore ice cream?

ar, ark, irt, ore, orn, urt

Name: _____

Silly Sentences

Circle the silly sentences. For each silly sentence you find, color the shape with that number. What picture do you see?

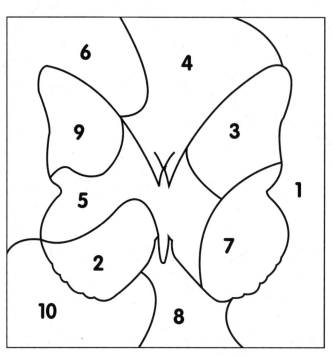

1. Is your name Mark?

2. I torn the margin on corn.

3. There are thorns in my horn.

4. My brother Clark was in the car.

5. His marble star is blurt.

6. Can I have more corn? I adore it!

7. My car pore is more sore than torn.

8. She wore a skirt to the store.

9. Unicorns were born from popcorn sharks.

10. It is fun to explore in the morning.

ar, ark, irt, ore, orn, urt

20 Week-by-Week Word Family Packets © 2008 by Lisa Fitzgerald McKeon Scholastic Teaching Resources

Name: _____

Read, Think, Then Read Again

Read the story below. Then color the activity that the shark and the star do <u>last</u>.

The Shark and the Star

First, the shark and the star go to the market.

Then, the shark gets popcorn.

Next, the star gets a toy car.

After that, they eat popcorn and play with the car in the dark.

ar, ark, irt, ore, orn, urt

Name: _____

Which Spelling Is Right?

Look at each picture. Then circle the correct spelling of the word.

1. stur
    ster
    star

2. sirt
    skurt
    skirt

3. corn
    acorn
    achorn

4. shar
    shark
    shrk

5. snor
    sore
    snore

6. hert
    hurt
    hirt

ar, ark, irt, ore, orn, urt

Name: ______________________________

Word Family Packet 19

You will learn these word families:

out, ouch, ound, ouse, ow, own

All of these families say "OW"!

ou + t → **spout**

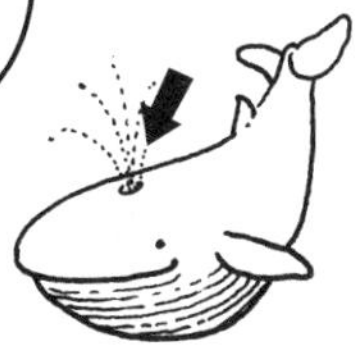

ou + ch → **couch**

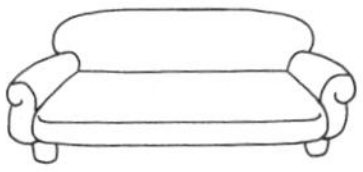

ou + nd → **playground**

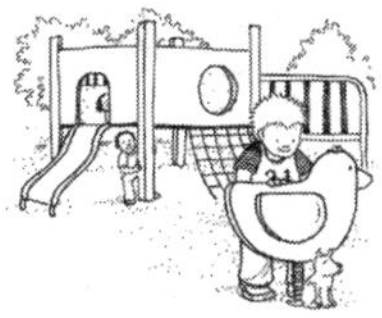

ou + se → **house**

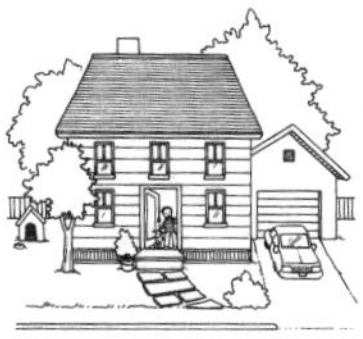

ow → **cow**

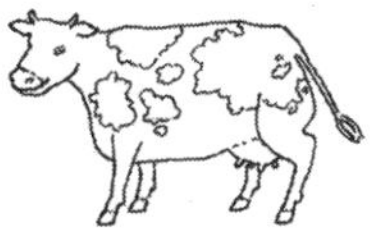

ow + n → **clown**

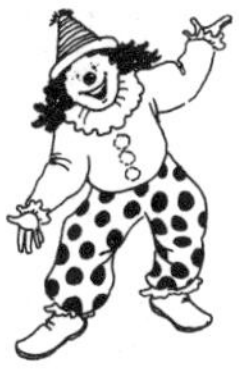

Checklist

✔ off each page after you complete it.

____ Activity 1

____ Activity 2

____ Activity 3

____ Activity 4

____ Activity 5

____ Activity 6

____ Activity 7

____ Activity 8

____ Activity 9

Name: _____

Which Words Live Here?

Use the letters and blends from the attic to make words in each word family. If you can't make any more real words, you can make nonsense words.

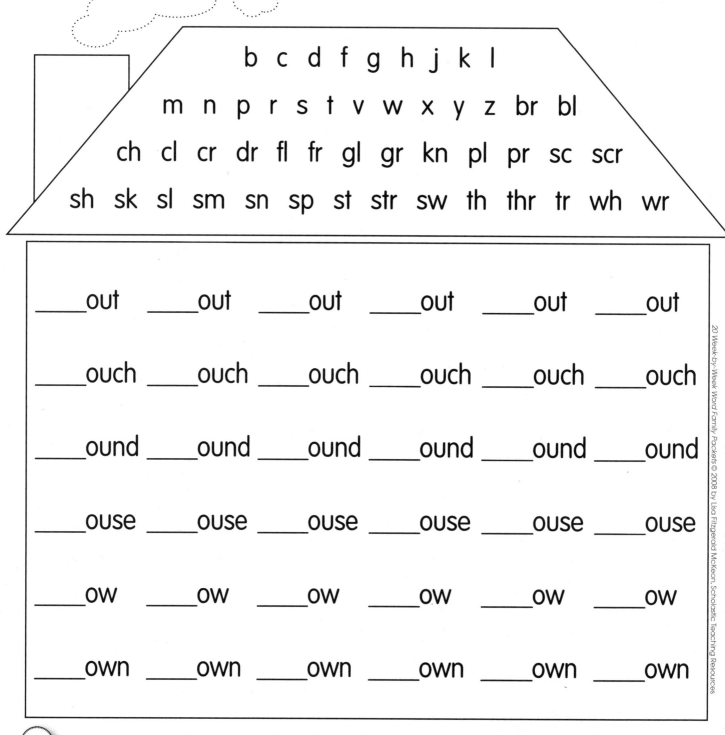

b c d f g h j k l

m n p r s t v w x y z br bl

ch cl cr dr fl fr gl gr kn pl pr sc scr

sh sk sl sm sn sp st str sw th thr tr wh wr

____out ____out ____out ____out ____out ____out

____ouch ____ouch ____ouch ____ouch ____ouch ____ouch

____ound ____ound ____ound ____ound ____ound ____ound

____ouse ____ouse ____ouse ____ouse ____ouse ____ouse

____ow ____ow ____ow ____ow ____ow ____ow

____own ____own ____own ____own ____own ____own

out, ouch, ound, ouse, ow, own

20 Week-by-Week Word Family Packets © 2008 by Lisa Fitzgerald McKeon, Scholastic Teaching Resources

Name: _____

Where Do You Hear It?

Do you hear the sound at the <u>B</u>EGINNING, <u>M</u>IDDLE, or <u>E</u>ND?
Circle the right answer.

1. I hear the **ch** in   at the   B   M   E

2. I hear the **s** in   at the   B   M   E

3. I hear the **l** in   at the   B   M   E

4. I hear the **c** in   at the   B   M   E

5. I hear the **sc** in   at the   B   M   E

6. I hear the **n** in   at the   B   M   E

7. I hear the **sh** in   at the   B   M   E

8. I hear the **n** in   at the   B   M   E

9. I hear the **bl** in   at the   B   M   E

10. I hear the **m** in   at the   B   M   E

out, ouch, ound, ouse, ow, own

Name: _____

How Many Sounds Can You Hear?

Put your hand on top of the hand below. Read each of the words out loud SLOWLY. For every sound you hear, tap on a finger. How many taps were there? Circle that number.

out	2	3	4	5
drown	2	3	4	5
ouch	2	3	4	5
how	2	3	4	5
pouch	2	3	4	5
round	2	3	4	5
spouts	2	3	4	5
anyhow	2	3	4	5
down	2	3	4	5

out, ouch, ound, ouse, ow, own

20 Week-by-Week Word Family Packets © 2008 by Lisa Fitzgerald McKeon, Scholastic Teaching Resources

Name: _____

Words From Earth or Mars?

Which words are real words we use on Earth? Which words are
Martian words used only on Mars? Sort them.

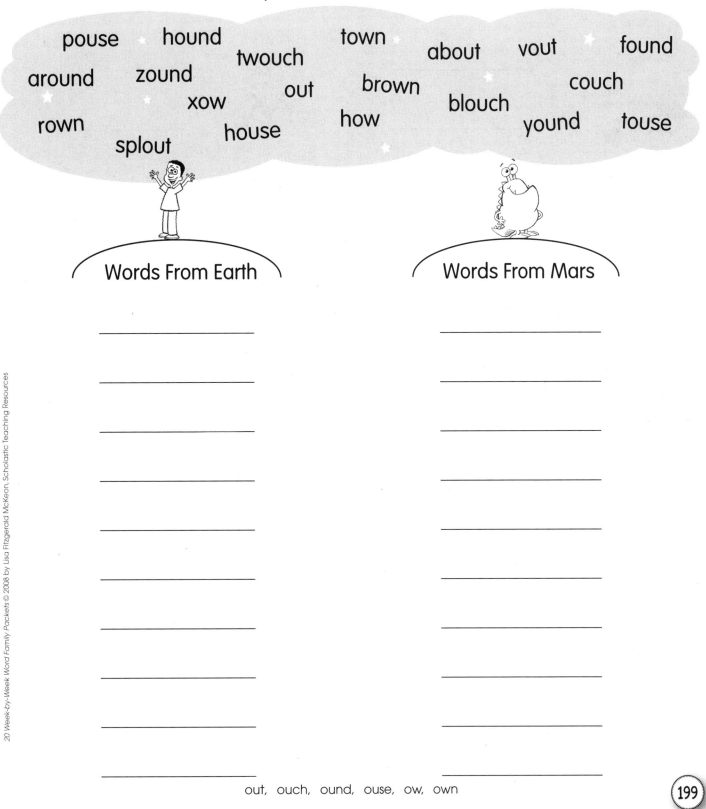

pouse   hound   town   about   vout   found

around   zound   twouch   brown   couch

rown   xow   out   blouch   young   touse

splout   house   how   yound

Words From Earth

Words From Mars

_____   _____

_____   _____

_____   _____

_____   _____

_____   _____

_____   _____

_____   _____

_____   _____

_____   _____

out, ouch, ound, ouse, ow, own

Name: _____

They All Sound the Same

Can you think of three rhyming words to go with each picture?

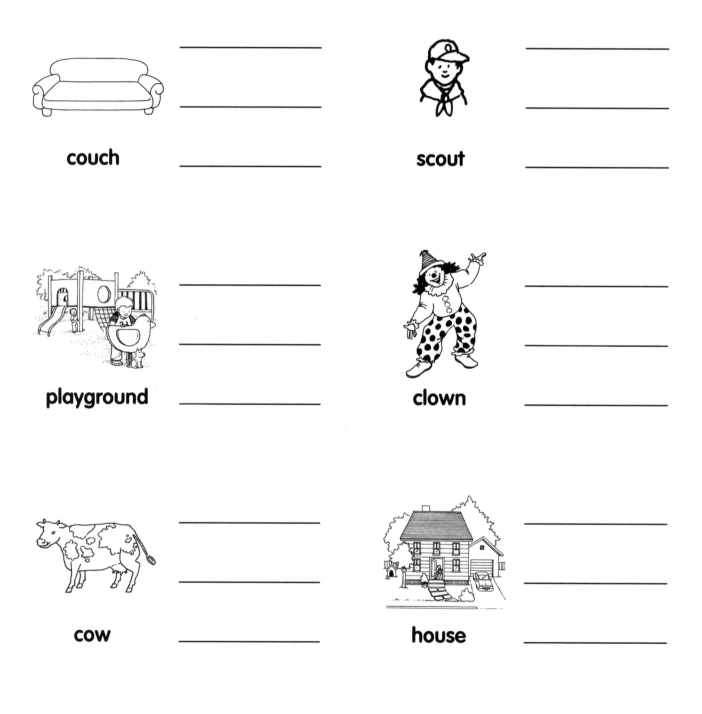

couch _____

scout _____

playground _____

clown _____

cow _____

house _____

out, ouch, ound, ouse, ow, own

20 Week-by-Week Word Family Packets © 2008 by Lisa Fitzgerald McKeon, Scholastic Teaching Resources

Name: _____

What Is Missing?

Complete the sentences by using each of the letters and blends from the magnifying glass.

m   br
n   sl
gr   tr

1. He fell on the ____ound and broke his arm.

2. We went fishing for some ____out.

3. The ____ouse ate some cheese.

4. ____own is my favorite color.

5. My mom always tells me not to ____ouch.

6. My dad said, "Come here right ____ow!"

out, ouch, ound, ouse, ow, own

Name: _____

Silly Sentences

Circle the silly sentences. For each silly sentence you find, color the shape with that number. What picture do you see?

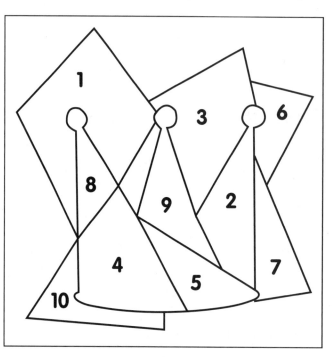

1. My teacher doesn't like it when I pout.

2. My eyebrow lives in a round doghouse.

3. The king had a gold crown.

4. Anyhow, her grouch is about.

5. The hound trout had a clown snout.

6. Grandma gave me a new nightgown.

7. I play with my friends on the playground outside.

8. Chow down your allowance right now!

9. The spout found a cow and a scout.

10. I like to play outside instead of sitting on the couch in my house.

out, ouch, ound, ouse, ow, own

Name: _____

Read, Think, Then Read Again

Read the story below. Then color the picture that goes with it.

The Cow

The cow does <u>not</u> sit on a couch.

The cow does <u>not</u> play with a round ball.

The cow does <u>not</u> stand near a house.

The cow does go to the playground.

out, ouch, ound, ouse, ow, own

Name: _____

Which Spelling Is Right?

Look at each picture. Then circle the correct spelling of the word.

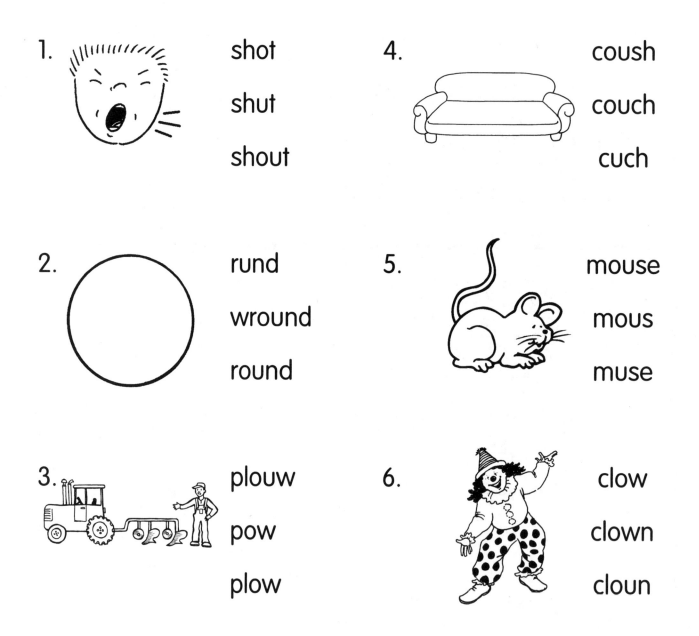

1. shot
   shut
   shout

4. coush
   couch
   cuch

2. rund
   wround
   round

5. mouse
   mous
   muse

3. plouw
   pow
   plow

6. clow
   clown
   cloun

out, ouch, ound, ouse, ow, own

Name: _____

You will learn these word families:
aw, awl, awn, all, aught, ought

All of these families say "AW"!

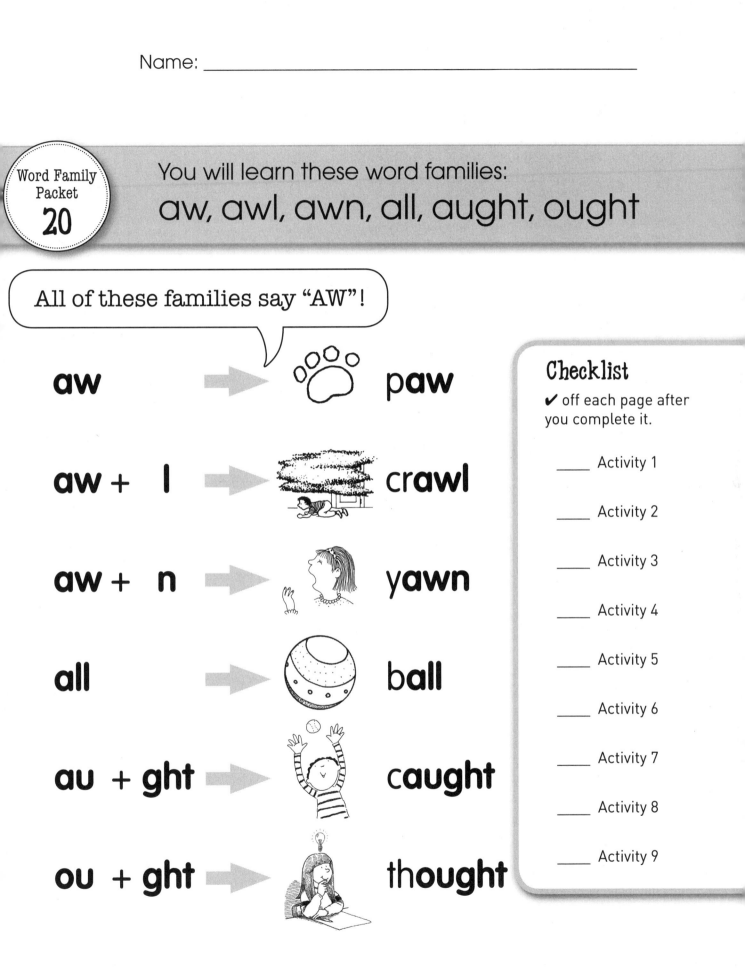

aw ➡️ p**aw**

aw + l ➡️ cr**awl**

aw + n ➡️ y**awn**

all ➡️ b**all**

au + ght ➡️ c**aught**

ou + ght ➡️ th**ought**

Checklist
✔ off each page after you complete it.

____ Activity 1

____ Activity 2

____ Activity 3

____ Activity 4

____ Activity 5

____ Activity 6

____ Activity 7

____ Activity 8

____ Activity 9

Name: _____

Which Words Live Here?

Use the letters and blends from the attic to make words in each word family. If you can't make any more real words, you can make nonsense words.

b c d f g h j k l

m n p r s t v w x y z br bl

ch cl cr dr fl fr gl gr kn pl pr sc scr

sh sk sl sm sn sp st str sw th thr tr wh wr

____aw   ____aw   ____aw   ____aw   ____aw   ____aw

____awl   ____awl   ____awl   ____awl   ____awl   ____awl

____awn   ____awn   ____awn   ____awn   ____awn   ____awz

____all   ____all   ____all   ____all   ____all   ____all

____aught ____aught ____aught ____aught ____aught ____aught

____ought ____ought ____ought ____ought ____ought ____ought

aw, awl, awn, all, aught, ought

20 Week-by-Week Word Family Packets © 2008 by Lisa Fitzgerald McKeon, Scholastic Teaching Resources

Name: _____

Where Do You Hear It?

Do you hear the sound at the <u>B</u>EGINNING, <u>M</u>IDDLE, or <u>E</u>ND?
Circle the right answer.

1. I hear the **l** in   at the   B   M   E

2. I hear the **y** in   at the   B   M   E

3. I hear the **aw** in   at the   B   M   E

4. I hear the **r** in   at the   B   M   E

5. I hear the **cl** in   at the   B   M   E

6. I hear the **aw** in   at the   B   M   E

7. I hear the **t** in   at the   B   M   E

8. I hear the **dr** in   at the   B   M   E

9. I hear the **th** in   at the   B   M   E

10. I hear the **k** in   at the   B   M   E

20 Week-by-Week Word Family Packets © 2008 by Lisa Fitzgerald McKeon, Scholastic Teaching Resources

aw, awl, awn, all, aught, ought

Name: _____

How Many Sounds Can You Hear?

Put your hand on top of the hand below. Read each of the words out loud SLOWLY. For every sound you hear, tap on a finger. How many taps were there? Circle that number.

raw	2	3	4	5
small	2	3	4	5
yawn	2	3	4	5
straw	2	3	4	5
shawl	2	3	4	5
bought	2	3	4	5
crawl	2	3	4	5
ball	2	3	4	5
caught	2	3	4	5

20 Week-by-Week Word Family Packets © 2008 by Lisa Fitzgerald McKeon, Scholastic Teaching Resources

aw, awl, awn, all, aught, ought

Name: _____

Words From Earth or Mars?

Which words are real words we use on Earth? Which words are Martian words used only on Mars? Sort them.

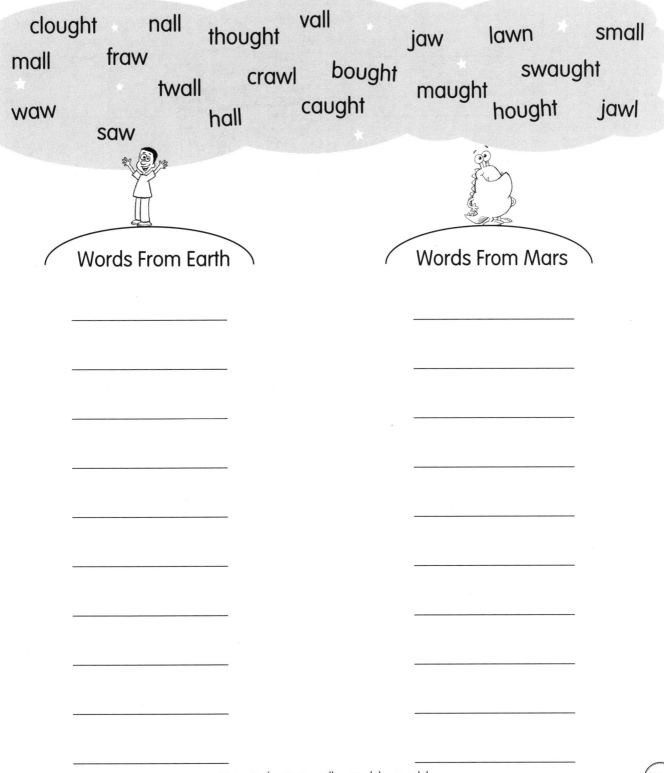

clought   nall   thought   vall   jaw   lawn   small

mall   fraw   crawl   bought   swaught

twall   maught

waw   caught   hought   jawl

saw   hall

Words From Earth   Words From Mars

_____   _____

_____   _____

_____   _____

_____   _____

_____   _____

_____   _____

_____   _____

_____   _____

_____   _____

aw, awl, awn, all, aught, ought

Name: _____

They All Sound the Same

Can you think of three rhyming words to go with each picture?

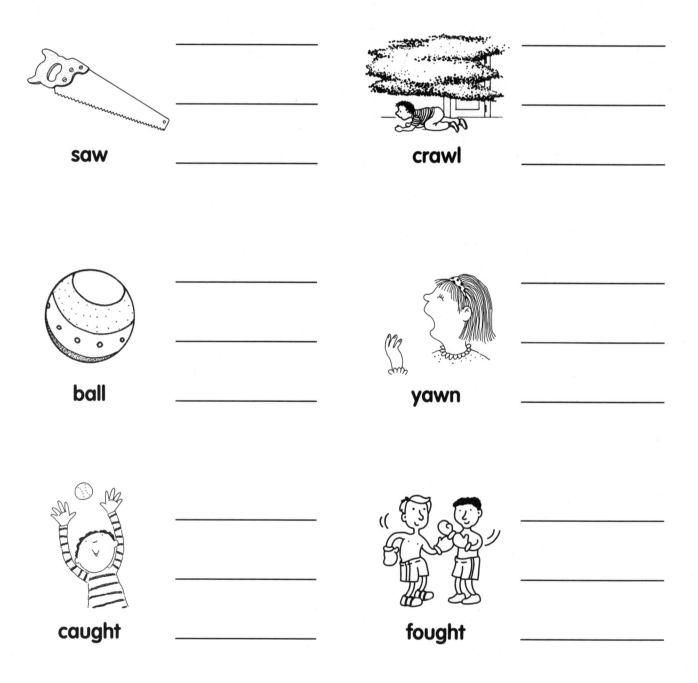

saw _____

crawl _____

ball _____

yawn _____

caught _____

fought _____

aw, awl, awn, all, aught, ought

Name: _____

What Is Missing?

Complete the sentences by using each of the letters and blends from the magnifying glass.

c   b

t   p

cr   l

1. Her baby sister learned to ____awl.

2. He is the ____allest boy in his class.

3. The grass on our ____awn grows very quickly.

4. She ____aught the ball with her left hand.

5. I taught my dog how to give me his _____aw.

6. At the store, I _____ought a new dress.

aw, awl, awn, all, aught, ought

211

Name: _____

Silly Sentences

Circle the silly sentences. For each silly sentence you find, color the shape with that number. What picture do you see?

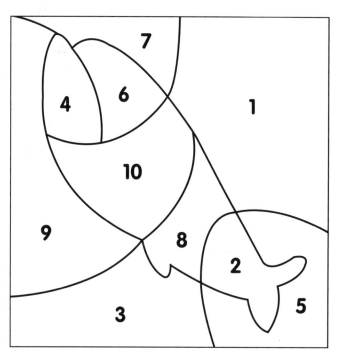

1. My jaw hurts.

2. Gnaw on this small hall.

3. I play on a small football team.

4. I fought the tall coleslaw.

5. I drank my soda with a straw.

6. Prawn his claw!

7. I caught the baseball.

8. An awning is on the mall shawl.

9. Her daughter is eighteen.

10. I will draw the yawn and then crawl in a waterfall.

aw, awl, awn, all, aught, ought

20 Week-by-Week Word Family Packets © 2008 by Lisa Fitzgerald McKeon Scholastic Teaching Resources

Name: _____

Read, Think, Then Read Again

Read the story below. Then color the activity that Paul does <u>last</u>.

A Day at the Mall

First, Paul went to the mall.

Then, he saw his tall pal.

Next, he bought a small ball.

After that, Paul and his pal played ball on the lawn.

aw, awl, awn, all, aught, ought

Name: _____

Which Spelling Is Right?

Look at each picture. Then circle the correct spelling of the word.

1. strw

    straw

    srtaw

4. crwal

    crawn

    crawl

2. jawn

    yawn

    wawn

5. smal

    smalle

    small

3. cauhgt

    cuaght

    caught

6. bought

    buohgt

    bouhgt

aw, awl, awn, all, aught, ought

Answer Key

Packet 1 (pages 15–24)

Activity 1: Answers will vary.

Activity 2: 1. E, 2. M, 3. B, 4. E, 5. E, 6. B, 7. B, 8. M, 9. E, 10. B

Activity 3: an = 2, bag = 3, cap = 3, mad = 3, flat = 4, cram = 4, at = 2, snaps = 5, chap = 3

Activity 4: Words from Earth: ram, plan, pad, that, lap, brag, flat, tan, slap, wag; words from Mars: zat, flad, bap, glap, smag, tam, crat, drad, gan, han

Activity 5: Answers will vary.

Activity 6: 1. cat, 2. ham, 3. van, 4. flag, 5. mad, 6. nap

Activity 7:

Activity 8: Picture #2 is correct.

Activity 9: 1. bat, 2. snap, 3. clam, 4. glad, 5. flag, 6. van

Packet 2 (pages 25–34)

Activity 1: Answers will vary.

Activity 2: 1. B, 2. E, 3. M, 4. B, 5. E, 6. M, 7. E, 8. E, 9. E, 10. M

Activity 3: ask = 3, champ = 4, cap = 3, quack = 3, damp = 4, bland = 5, can't = 4, ash = 2, flask = 5, land = 4

Activity 4: Words from Earth: smash, ask, flash, can't, champ, stack, back, sand, camp, plant; words from Mars: fant, jask, plash, wamp, grack, jand, pamp, twack, dand, sprask

Activity 5: Answers will vary.

Activity 6: 1. stamp, 2. mask, 3. hands, 4. plant, 5. snack, 6. rash

Activity 7:

Activity 8: Picture #4 is correct.

Activity 9: 1. stamp, 2. plant, 3. cash, 4. hand, 5. crack, 6. mask

Packet 3 (pages 35–44)

Activity 1: Answers will vary.

Activity 2: 1. B, 2. M, 3. E, 4. E, 5. M, 6. B, 7. E, 8. B, 9. B, 10. E

Activity 3: quit = 3, drip = 4, still = 4, big = 3, did = 3, split = 5, ill = 2, thrill = 4, thin = 3

Activity 4: Words from Earth: did, snip, split, thrill, thin, fill, chip, will, twig, tip; words from Mars: sig, chid, prill, mip, plip, gid, dit, nin, snig, flig

Activity 5: Answers will vary.

Activity 6: 1. slid, 2. lit, 3. chin, 4. big, 5. flip, 6. spill

Activity 7:

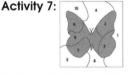

Activity 8: Picture #1 is correct.

Activity 9: 1. pin, 2. kid, 3. dig, 4. chin, 5. drip, 6. spill

Packet 4 (pages 45–54)

Activity 1: Answers will vary.

Activity 2: 1. B, 2. E, 3. B, 4. M, 5. B, 6. E, 7. B, 8. E, 9. M, 10. M

Activity 3: hint = 4, twist = 5, wish = 3, thick = 3, wing = 4, rink = 4, chick = 3, tick = 3, list = 4

Activity 4: Words from Earth: stink, list, pick, bring, blink, hint, wish, quick, fling, drink; words from Mars: zist, sish, crish, snint, mish, rint, gink, drist, smick, jing

Activity 5: Answers will vary.

Activity 6: 1. hint, 2. pink, 3. swing, 4. brick, 5. wish, 6. list

Activity 7:

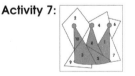

Activity 8: Picture #2 is correct.

Activity 9: 1. wrist, 2. swing, 3. fish, 4. drink, 5. sticks, 6. mint

Packet 5 (pages 55–64)

Activity 1: Answers will vary.

Activity 2: 1. B, 2. E, 3. M, 4. B, 5. E, 6. E, 7. B, 8. B, 9. M, 10. E

Activity 3: ox = 2, pod = 3, shop = 3, spot = 4, clog = 4, throb = 4, blot = 4, box = 3, robber = 4

Activity 4: Words from Earth: job, shop, nod, fog, dot, top, pop, flop, slob, box; words from Mars: spog, xot, chob, spog, thog, drot, swox, zob, twob, whot

Activity 5: Answers will vary.

Activity 6: 1. cob, 2. not, 3 jog, 4. fox, 5. rod, 6. shop

Activity 7:

Activity 8: Picture #2 is correct.

Activity 9: 1. knot, 2. fox, 3. rod, 4. drop, 5. jog, 6. sob

Packet 6 (pages 65–74)

Activity 1: Answers will vary.

Activity 2: 1. B, 2. E, 3. E, 4. M, 5. B, 6. M, 7. B and E, 8. B, 9. E, 10. B

Activity 3: wrong = 4, lock = 3, fond = 4, toss = 3, clock = 4, long = 4, frost = 5, moth = 3, cloth = 4

Activity 4: Words from Earth: blond, moth, wrong, long, boss, floss, shock, frost, block, cloth; words from Mars: jond, woss, swond, poth, goss, xoth, plong, zost, wock, vong

Activity 5: Answers will vary.

Activity 6: 1. broth, 2, stong, 3. lost, 4. floss, 5. pond, 6. tock

Activity 7: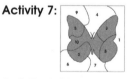

Activity 8: Picture #1 is correct.

Activity 9: 1. pond, 2. clock, 3. toss, 4. song, 5. moth, 6. frost

Packet 7 (pages 75–84)

Activity 1: Answers will vary.

Activity 2: 1. M, 2. E, 3. E, 4. M, 5. B, 6. M, 7. B, 8. E, 9. B, 10. E

Activity 3: wet = 3, sled = 4, chess = 3, beg =3, shed = 3, shred = 4, when = 3, swell = 4, yet = 3

Activity 4: Words from Earth: when, beg, then, red, yell, yet, wet, spell, fell, mess; words from Mars: speg, hess, twen, sket, cren, ged, zet, lell, plet, teg

Activity 5: Answers will vary.

Activity 6: 1. mess, 2. pet, 3. bed, 4. spell, 5. leg, 6. ten

Activity 7:

Activity 8: Picture #2 is correct.

Activity 9: 1. upset, 2. shed, 3. dress, 4. pen, 5. leg, 6. smell

Packet 8 (pages 85–94)

Activity 1: Answers will vary.

Activity 2: 1. E, 2. E, 3. B, 4. B, 5. M, 6. B, 7. M, 8. B, 9. M, 10. B

Activity 3: end = 3, wrench = 4, dent = 4, felt = 4, check = 3, best = 4, sent = 4, tend = 4, quench = 4

Activity 4: Words from Earth: felt, peck, French, spent, went, rest, bench, dent, best, pest; words from Mars: zend, meck, splench, flend, weck, clent, vench, kest, strelt, jelt

Activity 5: Answers will vary.

Activity 6: 1. sent, 2. wrench, 3. lend, 4. felt, 5. best, 6. neck

Activity 7:

Activity 8: Picture #4 is correct.

Activity 9: 1. bend, 2. dent, 3. check, 4. belt, 5. chest, 6. bench

Packet 9 (pages 95–104)

Activity 1: Answers will vary.

Activity 2: 1. B, 2. E, 3. M, 4. B, 5. E, 6. M, 7. E, 8. B, 9. M, 10. B

Activity 3: up = 2, chug = 3, gun = 3, shut = 3, swum = 4, plus = 4, chum = 3, shrug =4, us = 2

Activity 4: Words from Earth: nut, drum, plus, fun, cup, bus, spun, pup, shut, rug; words from Mars: wut, gurn, zus, lup, shus, chun, bup, twum, flun, dup

Activity 5: Answers will vary.

Activity 6: 1. nut, 2. mugs, 3. gum, 4. pup, 5. plus, 6. run

Activity 7:

Activity 8: Picture #1 is correct.

Activity 9: 1. run, 2. cup, 3. drum, 4. nut, 5. bus, 6. plug

Packet 10 (pages 105–114)

Activity 1: Answers will vary.

Activity 2: 1. E, 2. B, 3. M, 4. E, 5. M, 6. M, 7. E, 8. M, 9. B, 10. B

Activity 3: junk = 4, flung = 5, gush = 3, rust = 4, pump = 4, chuck = 3, chunk = 4, blush = 4, rush = 3

Activity 4: Words from Earth = just, luck, must, lung, stung, grump, stuck, rush, junk, lump; words from Mars = yunk, grust, snust, juck, gung, wush, vump, gruck, twust, zunk

Activity 5: Answers will vary.

Activity 6: 1. jump, 2. lung, 3. crust, 4. truck, 5. rush 6. bunk

Activity 7:

Activity 8: Picture #3 is correct.

Activity 9: 1. jump, 2. brush, 3. lungs, 4. crust, 5. skunk, 6. truck

Packet 11 (pages 115–124)

Activity 1: Answers will vary.

Activity 2: 1. E, 2. M, 3. B, 4. B, 5. B, 6. E, 7. B, 8. E, 9. M, 10. E

Activity 3: shape = 3, blame = 4, fake = 3, crate = 4, whale = 3, ape = 2, state = 4, scrape = 5, came = 3

Activity 4: from Earth: same, save, brave, make, sale, late, behave, cape, bake, shape; words from Mars: vape, gake, twame, spave, zate, dake, prale, clale, chame, wape

Activity 5: Answers will vary.

Activity 6: 1. whale, 2. same, 3. gate, 4. shave, 5. pancakes, 6. scrape

Activity 7:

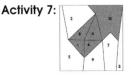

Activity 8: Picture #1 is correct.

Activity 9: 1. snake, 2. frame, 3. paper, 4. whale, 5. plate, 6. cave

Packet 12 (pages 125–134)

Activity 1: Answers will vary.

Activity 2: 1. E, 2. M, 3. E, 4. E, 5. B, 6. E, 7. B, 8. B, 9. E, 10. B

Activity 3: spray = 4, chain = 3, thank = 4, sang = 4, hay = 2, gang = 4, bank = 4, eight = 2, weigh = 2

Activity 4: Words from Earth: spray, weigh, snail, faint, tray, jail, train, drank, fang, bank; words from Mars: splain, snay, prain, creigh, brang, xlain, thay, smank, tway, zail

Activity 5: Answers will vary.

Activity 6: 1. mailbox, 2. stank, 3. rain, 4. hanging, 5. weigh, 6. say

Activity 7:

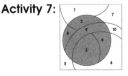

Activity 8: Picture #4 is correct.

Activity 9: 1. tray, 2. mail, 3. sleigh, 4. paint, 5. sang, 6. drank

Packet 13 (pages 135–144)

Activity 1: Answers will vary.

Activity 2: 1. E, 2. E, 3. E, 4. M, 5. B, 6. M, 7. M, 8. B, 9. B, 10. E

Activity 3: chose = 3, poke = 3, open = 4, alone = 4, whole = 3, stroke = 5, over = 3, drove = 4, slope = 4

Activity 4: Words from Earth: stole, open, stroke, those, nope, spoke, alone, phone, joke, drove; words from Mars: crole, chone, zole, twove, zope, wose, crove, whope, vose, boke

Activity 5: Answers will vary.

Activity 6: 1. chose, 2. jokes, 3. stove, 4. mole, 5. hope, 6. bone

Activity 7:

Activity 8: Picture #3 is correct.

Activity 9: 1. rope, 2. clover, 3. nose, 4. smoke, 5. bone, 6. pole

Packet 14 (pages 145–154)

Activity 1: Answers will vary.

Activity 2: 1. E, 2. E, 3. M, 4. E, 5. B, 6. E, 7. B, 8. M, 9. M, 10. B

Activity 3: coach = 3, old = 3, hero = 4, know = 2, no = 2, throat = 4, roach = 3, older = 4, window = 5

Activity 4: Words from Earth: no, float, blow, cold, know, load, boat, toad, so, fold; words from Mars: dro, chone, splo, po, smoad, stroat, spold, wold, pload, zo

Activity 5: Answers will vary.

Activity 6: 1. fold, 2. coach, 3. toad, 4. rows, 5. no, 6. float

Activity 7:

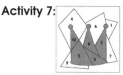

Activity 8: Picture #2 is correct.

Activity 9: 1. snow, 2. road, 3. volcano, 4. throat, 5. cold, 6. coach

Packet 15 (pages 155–164)

Activity 1: Answers will vary.

Activity 2: 1. E, 2. M, 3. M, 4. E, 5. B, 6. E, 7. E, 8. E, 9. M, 10. B

Activity 3: glide = 4, ice = 2, shine = 3, knight = 3, tighter = 4, side = 3, sky = 3, write = 3, my = 2

Activity 4: Words from Earth: pride, fine, dry, twice, slice, bright, flight, wide, white, line; words from Mars: hice, kice, splight, wy, stice, bine, gry, gight, swite, snite

Activity 5: Answers will vary.

Activity 6: 1. line, 2. hide, 3. night 4. bite, 5. rice, 6. fly

Activity 7:

Activity 8: Picture #1 is correct.

Activity 9: 1. spider, 2. nine, 3. write, 4. price, 5. night, 6. eye

Packet 16 (pages 165–174)

Activity 1: Answers will vary.

Activity 2: 1. E, 2. E, 3. E, 4. M, 5. B, 6. B, 7. B, 8. B, 9. B, 10. B

Activity 3: pleat = 4, sheep = 3, see = 2, teacher = 4, seat = 3, squeal = 4, agree = 4, cream = 4, reach = 3

Activity 4: Words from Earth: tree, cheat, sheep, creep, reach, dream, steal, neat, free, scream; words form Mars: weach, spearn, creal, mee, sneat, hee, geal, fleach, screep, zeat

Activity 5: Answers will vary.

Activity 6: 1. seal, 2. treat, 3. beach, 4. three, 5. jeep, 6. dream

Activity 7:

Activity 8: Picture #3 is correct.

Activity 9: 1. seal, 2. sweep, 3. sixteen, 4. neat, 5. teacher, 6. dream

Packet 17 (pages 175–184)

Activity 1: Answers will vary.

Activity 2: 1. E, 2. B, 3. E, 4. E, 5. E, 6. B, 7. M, 8. E, 9. B, 10. E

Activity 3: flute = 4, drool = 4, use = 2, noon = 3, value = 4, reuse = 4, true = 3, soon = 3, threw = 3

Activity 4: Words from Earth: school, true, cute, few, soon, used, flute, fool, new, clue; words from Mars: guse, swute, dwool, zool, tew, tuse, dute, grue, buse, snew

Activity 5: Answers will vary.

Activity 6: 1. flute, 2. moon, 3. pool, 4. new, 5. blue, 6. used

Activity 7:

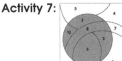

Activity 8: Picture #4 is correct.

Activity 9: 1. screw, 2. cute, 3. school, 4. glue, 5. confused, 6. spoon

Packet 18 (pages 185–194)

Activity 1: Answers will vary.

Activity 2: 1. M, 2. B, 3. B, 4. E, 5. M, 6. M, 7. M, 8. B, 9. B, 10. M

Activity 3: star = 3, acorn = 4, hurt = 3, store = 3, spark = 4, skirt = 4, born = 3, dirt = 3, dirty = 4

Activity 4: Words form Earth: more, shark, hurt, store, scar, thorn, spark, snore, shirt, star; words from Mars: qark, brar, har, swurt, rirt, blore, jurt, var, yorn, xark

Activity 5: Answers will vary.

Activity 6: 1. hurt, 2. corn, 3. star, 4. park, 5. shirt, 6. more

Activity 7:

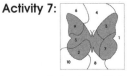

Activity 8: Picture #1 is correct.

Activity 9: 1. star, 2. skirt, 3. acorn, 4. shark, 5. snore, 6. hurt

Packet 19 (pages 195–204)

Activity 1: Answers will vary.

Activity 2: 1. E, 2. E, 3. B, 4. B, 5. B, 6. E, 7. B, 8. E, 9. B, 10. B

Activity 3: out = 2, drown = 4, ouch = 2, how = 2, pouch = 3, round = 4, spouts = 5, anyhow = 5, down = 3

Activity 4: Words from Earth: found, around, hound, town, brown, out, how, about, couch, house; words from Mars: pouse, rown, splout, xow, zound, twouch, blouch, vout, yound, touse

Activity 5: Answers will vary.

Activity 6: 1. ground, 2. trout, 3. mouse, 4. brown, 5. slouch, 6. now

Activity 7:

Activity 8: Picture #2 is correct.

Activity 9: 1. shout, 2. round, 3. plow, 4. couch, 5. mouse, 6. clown

Packet 20 (pages 205–214)

Activity 1: Answers will vary.

Activity 2: 1. E, 2. B, 3. M, 4. M, 5. M, 6. E, 7. B, 8. B, 9. B, 10. E

Activity 3: raw = 2, small = 4, yawn = 3, straw = 4, shawl = 3, bought = 3, crawl = 4, ball = 3, caught = 3

Activity 4: Words from Earth: mall, saw, thought, crawl, hall, bought, caught, jaw, lawn, small; words from Mars: clought, waw, fraw, nall, twall, vall, maught, swaught, hought, jawl.

Activity 5: Answers will vary.

Activity 6: 1. crawl, 2. tallest, 3. lawn, 4. caught, 5. paw, 6. bought

Activity 7:

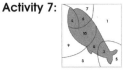

Activity 8: Picture #1 is correct.

Activity 9: 1. straw, 2. yawn, 3. caught, 4. crawl, 5. small, 6. bought

Word Family Lists

Packet 1

-at
bat
cat
fat
gnat
hat
mat
pat
rat
sat
vat
brat
chat
flat
scat
slat
spat
that

-ad
bad
dad
fad
had
lad
mad
pad
sad
tad
Brad
clad
glad

-ap
cap
gap
lap
map
nap
rap
sap
tap
yap
chap
clap
flap
scrap
slap
snap
strap
trap
wrap

-ag
bag
gag
lag
nag
rag
sag

tag
wag
brag
crag
drag
flag
shag
snag
stag

-am
cam
dam
ham
jam
Pam
ram
Sam
tam
yam
clam
cram
gram
scam
scram
sham
slam
swam

-an
an
ban
can
Dan
fan
man
pan
ran
tan
van
bran
clan
Fran
plan
scan
span
than

Packet 2

-amp
camp
damp
lamp
ramp
vamp
champ
clamp
cramp
scamp
stamp
tramp

-and
and
band
hand
land
sand
bland
brand
gland
stand
strand

-ant
ant
pant
rant
chant
grant
plant
scant
slant

-ack
back
hack
Jack
lack
Mack
pack
quack
rack
sack
tack
black
clack
crack
knack
shack
slack
smack
snack
stack
track
whack

-ash
bash
cash
dash
gash
hash
lash
mash
rash
sash
brash
clash
flash
slash
smash
stash

trash
thrash

-ask
ask
cask
mask
task
flask

Packet 3

-it
bit
fit
hit
kit
knit
lit
pit
quit
sit
wit
flit
grit
skit
slit
spit
split

-in
bin
fin
kin
pin
tin
win
chin
grin
shin
skin
spin
thin
twin

-id
bid
did
hid
kid
lid
mid
rid
grid
skid
slid
squid

-ip
dip
hip
lip

nip
quip
rip
sip
tip
zip
blip
chip
clip
drip
flip
grip
ship
skip
slip
snip
trip
whip
strip

-ig
big
dig
fig
gig
jig
pig
rig
wig
brig
swig
twig
sprig

-ill
ill
bill
dill
fill
gill
hill
Jill
kill
mill
pill
quill
sill
till
will
chill
drill
frill
grill
skill
spill
still
trill
twill
thrill

Packet 4

-int
hint
lint
mint
tint
glint
print
stint
splint
sprint
squint

-ist
fist
list
mist
wrist
twist

-ink
ink
kink
link
mink
pink
rink
sink
wink
blink
brink
clink
drink
slink
stink
think
shrink

-ing
ding
king
ping
ring
sing
wing
zing
bring
cling
fling
sling
string
swing
thing
wring
sting
spring

-ick
kick
lick
Nick
pick
quick
Rick

sick
tick
wick
brick
chick
click
flick
slick
thick
trick

-ish
dish
fish
wish
swish

Packet 5
-ot
cot
dot
got
hot
jot
knot
lot
not
pot
rot
tot
blot
clot
plot
shot
slot
spot
trot

-op
bop
cop
hop
mop
pop
sop
top
chop
crop
drop
flop
plop
prop
shop
slop
stop

-ox
ox
box
fox
lox
pox

-og
bog
dog
fog
hog
jog
log
clog
frog
smog

-ob
bob
cob
gob
job
knob
lob
mob
rob
sob
blob
glob
slob
snob
throb

-od
cod
nod
pod
rod
sod
plod
prod
trod

Packet 6
-ond
bond
fond
pond
blond

-ong
gong
long
song
strong
wrong

-ock
dock
hock
knock
lock
mock
rock
sock
tock
block
clock
crock
flock
frock

knock
shock
smock
stock

-oth
moth
broth
cloth
froth
sloth

-oss
boss
loss
moss
toss
Ross
cross
floss
gloss

-ost
cost
lost
frost

Packet 7
-et
bet
get
jet
let
met
net
pet
set
wet
yet
Chet
fret

-en
Ben
den
hen
Ken
men
pen
ten
yen
glen
then
when
wren

-ed
bed
fed
led
Ned
red
Ted
wed
bled

bred
fled
Fred
shed
sled
sped
shred

-eg
beg
keg
leg
Meg
peg

-ess
Bess
guess
less
mess
bless
chess
dress
press
stress

-ell
bell
cell
dell
fell
Nell
sell
tell
well
yell
dwell
shell
smell
spell
swell

Packet 8
-end
end
bend
fend
lend
mend
send
tend
blend
spend
trend

-elt
belt
felt
melt
pelt
welt
dwelt
knelt

-ent
bent
cent
dent
gent
Kent
lent
rent
sent
tent
vent
went
scent
spent

-est
best
jest
lest
nest
pest
rest
test
vest
west
zest
chest
crest
quest

-eck
deck
heck
neck
peck
check
fleck
speck
wreck

-ench
bench
clench
drench
French
quench
stench
trench
wrench

Packet 9
-ug
bug
dug
hug
jug
lug
mug
pug
rug
tug
chug
drug
plug

slug
smug
snug
thug
shrug

-um
bum
gum
hum
mum
sum
chum
drum
glum
plum
scum
slum
swum
strum

-un
bun
fun
run
sun
shun
spun
stun

-us
bus
plus
thus

-up
cup
pup
sup

-ut
but
cut
gut
hut
jut

nut
glut
shut
strut

Packet 10
-ump
bump
dump
hump
jump
lump
pump
rump
chump
clump
frump

grump
plump
slump
stump
thump
trump

-ust
bust
dust
gust
just
must
rust
crust
thrust
trust

-ush
gush
hush
lush
mush
rush
blush
brush
crush
flush
plush
slush
thrush

-unk
bunk
dunk
hunk
junk
sunk
chunk
drunk
flunk
plunk
shrunk
stunk
trunk

-ung
hung
lung
rung
sung
clung
flung
stung
swung
wrung
sprung

-uck
buck
duck
luck
muck
puck

suck
tuck
chuck
cluck
pluck
stuck
truck
struck

Packet 11
-ake
bake
cake
fake
Jake
lake
make
quake
rake
sake
take
wake
brake
drake
flake
shake
snake
stake

-ale
bale
dale
gale
male
pale
sale
tale
scale
stale
whale

-ame
came
dame
fame
game
lame
name
same
tame
blame
flame
frame
shame

-ate
date
fate
hate
Kate
late
mate
rate
crate

grate
plate
skate
state

-ape
cape
gape
nape
tape
drape
grape
shape
scrape

-ave
cave
Dave
gave
pave
rave
save
wave
brave
crave
grave
shave
slave

Packet 12
-ay
bay
day
gay
hay
jay
lay
may
nay
pay
ray
say
way
clay
gray
play
pray
slay
stay
sway
tray
spray
stray

-ain
main
pain
rain
vain
brain
chain
drain
grain
plain

slain
Spain
train
sprain
stain
strain

-ail
bail
fail
Gail
hail
jail
mail
nail
pail
quail
rail
sail
tail
wail
flail
frail
snail
trail

-ank
bank
dank
rank
sank
yank
blank
clank
crank
drank
frank
plank
prank
thank

-ang
bang
fang
gang
hang
rang
sang
tang
slang
sprang
twang

-eigh
neigh
weigh
sleigh

Packet 13
-ope
cope
dope
hope
mope

nope
pope
rope
scope
slope

-oke
Coke
joke
poke
woke
yoke
broke
choke
smoke
spoke
stoke
stroke

-ove
cove
rove
wove
clove
drove
grove
stove
trove

-one
bone
cone
hone
lone
tone
zone
clone
drone
phone
prone
shone
stone

-ose
hose
nose
pose
rose
chose
close
prose
those

-ole
dole
hole
mole
pole
role
stole
whole

Packet 14
-ow
bow

low
mow
row
sow
tow
blow
crow
flow
glow
grow
know
show
slow
snow
stow
throw

-oat
oat
boat
coat
goat
moat
bloat
float
gloat
throat

-oad
load
road
toad

-old
old
bold
cold
fold
gold
hold

mold
sold
told
scold

-o
go
no
so
pro

-oach
coach
poach
roach
broach

Packet 15
-ide
hide
ride
side
tide

wide
bride
glide
pride
slide
snide
stride

-ice
dice
lice
mice
nice
rice
vice
price
slice
spice
twice

-ine
dine
fine
line
mine
nine
pine
vine
wine
shine
spine
swine
whine
shrine

-ight
fight
knight
light
might
night
right
sight
tight
bright
flight
plight
slight

-ite
bite
kite
mite
quite
rite
site
white
write
sprite

-y
by
my
cry
dry
fly
fry
ply
pry
shy
sky
sly
spy
try
why

Packet 16
-eat
eat
beat
feat
heat
meat
neat
peat
seat
bleat
cheat
cleat
pleat
treat
wheat

-each
beach
leach
peach
reach
teach
bleach
breach
preach

-eal
deal
heal
meal
peal
real
seal
teal
veal
zeal
squeal
steal

-eep
beep
deep
jeep
keep
peep
seep

223

weep
cheep
creep
sheep
sleep
steep
sweep

-eam
beam
ream
seam
team
cream
dream
gleam
steam
stream
scream

-ee
bee
fee
knee
Lee
see
tee
wee
flee
free
glee
tree
spree
three

Packet 17
-ew
dew
few
knew
mew
new
pew
brew
blew
stew
drew
chew
crew
flew
knew
grew
screw
threw

-ue
cue
due
hue
Sue
blue
clue
glue
true

-ute
cute
lute
mute
brute
chute
flute

-use
use
fuse
muse
ruse

-ool
cool
fool
pool
tool
drool
spool
stool
school

-oon
boon
loon
moon
noon
soon
croon
spoon
swoon

Packet 18
-ar
bar
car
far
jar
mar
tar
char
scar
spar
star

-ark
bark
dark
hark
lark
mark
park
Clark
spark
stark

-irt
dirt
flirt
shirt
skirt
squirt

-ore
bore
core
gore
more
pore
sore
tore
wore
chore
score
shore
snore
spore
store
swore

-orn
born
corn
horn
morn
torn
worn
scorn
sworn
thorn

-urt
curt
hurt
blurt
spurt

Packet 19
-out
out
bout
pout
clout
scout
shout
snout
spout
stout
trout
sprout

-ouch
couch
pouch
vouch
crouch
grouch
slouch

-ound
bound
found
hound
mound
pound
round

sound
wound
ground

-ouse
house
louse
mouse
blouse
spouse

-ow
bow
cow
how
now
sow
vow
brow
chow
plow

-own
down
gown
town
brown
clown
crown
drown
frown

Packet 20
-aw
caw
gnaw
jaw
law
paw
raw
saw
claw
draw
flaw
slaw
thaw
squaw
straw

-awl
bawl
brawl
crawl
drawl
shawl
scrawl

-awn
dawn
fawn
lawn
pawn
yawn
brawn

drawn
prawn

-all
all
ball
call
fall
hall
mall
tall
wall
small
stall
squall

-aught
caught
naught
taught
fraught

-ought
ought
bought
fought
sought
brought
thought